TOUCHSTONE

MICHAEL MCCARTHY
JEANNE MCCARTEN
HELEN SANDIFORD

STUDENT'S BOOK

CAMBRIDGE UNIVERSITY PRESS
Cambridge, New York, Melbourne, Madrid, Cape Town, Singapore, São Paulo, Delhi

Cambridge University Press
32 Avenue of the Americas, New York, NY 10013-2473, USA

www.cambridge.org
Information on this title: www.cambridge.org/9780521601450

First published 2006
2nd printing 2009

Printed in Hong Kong, China, by Golden Cup Printing Company, Limited

A catalog record for this publication is available from the British Library

ISBN 978-0-521-66593-3 pack consisting of student's book and self-study audio CD/CD-ROM (Windows®, Mac®)
ISBN 978-0-521-60144-3 pack consisting of student's book/Korea and self-study audio CD/CD-ROM (Windows®, Mac®)
ISBN 978-0-521-60145-0 pack consisting of student's book A and self-study audio CD/CD-ROM (Windows®, Mac®)
ISBN 978-0-521-60146-7 pack consisting of student's book B and self-study audio CD/CD-ROM (Windows®, Mac®)
ISBN 978-0-521-66592-6 workbook
ISBN 978-0-521-60147-4 workbook A
ISBN 978-0-521-60148-1 workbook B
ISBN 978-0-521-66591-9 teacher's edition
ISBN 978-0-521-66588-9 CDs (audio)
ISBN 978-0-521-66589-6 cassettes

Art direction, book design, photo research, and layout services: Adventure House, NYC
Audio production: Full House, NYC

Authors' acknowledgments

Touchstone has benefited from extensive development research. The authors and publishers would like to extend their particular thanks to the following reviewers, consultants, and piloters for their valuable insights and suggestions.

Reviewers and consultants:

Thomas Job Lane and Marilia de M. Zanella from **Associação Alumni**, São Paulo, Brazil; Simon Banha from **Phil Young's English School**, Curitiba, Brazil; Katy Cox from **Casa Thomas Jefferson**, Brasilia, Brazil; Rodrigo Santana from **CCBEU**, Goiânia, Brazil; Cristina Asperti, Nancy H. Lake, and Airton Pretini Junior from **CEL LEP**, São Paulo, Brazil; Sonia Cury from **Centro Britânico**, São Paulo, Brazil; Daniela Alves Meyer from **IBEU**, Rio de Janeiro, Brazil; Ayeska Farias from **Mai English**, Belo Horizonte, Brazil; Solange Cassiolato from **LTC**, São Paulo, Brazil; Fernando Prestes Maia from **Polidiomas**, São Paulo, Brazil; Chris Ritchie and Debora Schisler from **Seven Idiomas**, São Paulo, Brazil; Maria Teresa Maiztegui and Joacyr de Oliveira from **União Cultural EEUU**, São Paulo, Brazil; Sakae Onoda from **Chiba University of Commerce**, Ichikawa, Japan; James Boyd and Ann Conlon from **ECC Foreign Language Institute**, Osaka, Japan; Catherine Chamier from **ELEC**, Tokyo, Japan; Janaka Williams, Japan; David Aline from **Kanagawa University**, Yokohama, Japan; Brian Long from **Kyoto University of Foreign Studies**, Kyoto, Japan; Alistair Home and Brian Quinn from **Kyushu University**, Fukuoka, Japan; Rafael Dovale from **Matsushita Electric Industrial Co., Ltd.**, Osaka, Japan; Bill Acton, Michael Herriman, Bruce Monk, and Alan Thomson from **Nagoya University of Commerce**, Nisshin, Japan; Alan Bessette from **Poole Gakuin University**, Osaka, Japan; Brian Collins from **Sundai Foreign Language Institute, Tokyo College of Music**, Tokyo, Japan; Todd Odgers from **The Tokyo Center for Language and Culture**, Tokyo, Japan; Jion Hanagata from **Tokyo Foreign Language College**, Tokyo, Japan; Peter Collins and Charlene Mills from **Tokai University**, Hiratsuka, Japan; David Stewart from **Tokyo Institute of Technology**, Tokyo, Japan; Alberto Peto Villalobos from **Cenlex Santo Tomás**, Mexico City, Mexico; Diana Jones and Carlos Lizarraga from **Instituto Angloamericano**, Mexico City, Mexico; Raúl Mar and María Teresa Monroy from **Universidad de Cuautitlán Izcalli**, Mexico City, Mexico; JoAnn Miller from **Universidad del Valle de México**, Mexico City, Mexico; Orlando Carranza from **ICPNA**, Peru; Sister Melanie Bair and Jihyeon Jeon from **The Catholic University of Korea**, Seoul, South Korea; Peter E. Nelson from **Chung-Ang University**, Seoul, South Korea; Joseph Schouweiler from **Dongguk University**, Seoul, South Korea; Michael Brazil and Sean Witty from **Gwangwoon University**, Seoul, South Korea; Kelly Martin and Larry Michienzi from **Hankook FLS University**, Seoul, South Korea; Scott Duerstock and Jane Miller from **Konkuk University**, Seoul, South Korea; Athena Pichay from **Korea University**, Seoul, South Korea; Lane Darnell Bahl, Susan Caesar, and Aaron Hughes from **Korea University**, Seoul, South Korea; Farzana Hyland and Stephen van Vlack from **Sookmyung Women's University**, Seoul, South Korea; Hae-Young Kim, Terry Nelson, and Ron Schafrick from **Sungkyunkwan University**, Seoul, South Korea; Mary Chen and Michelle S. M. Fan from **Chinese Cultural University**, Taipei, Taiwan; Joseph Sorell from **Christ's College**, Taipei, Taiwan; Dan Aldridge and Brian Kleinsmith from **ELSI**, Taipei, Taiwan; Ching-Shyang Anna Chien and Duen-Yeh Charles Chang from **Hsin Wu Institute of Technology**, Taipei, Taiwan; Timothy Hogan, Andrew Rooney, and Dawn Young from **Language Training and Testing Center**, Taipei, Taiwan; Jen Mei Hsu and Yu-hwei Eunice Shih from **National Taiwan Normal University**, Taipei, Taiwan; Roma Starczewska and Su-Wei Wang from **PQ3R Taipei Language and Computer Center**, Taipei, Taiwan; Elaine Paris from **Shih Chien University**, Taipei, Taiwan; Jennifer Castello from **Cañada College**, Redwood City, California, USA; Dennis Johnson, Gregory Keech, and Penny Larson from **City College of San Francisco – Institute for International Students**, San Francisco, California, USA; Ditra Henry from **College of Lake County**, Gray's Lake, Illinois, USA; Madeleine Murphy from **College of San Mateo**, San Mateo, California, USA; Ben Yoder from **Harper College**, Palatine, Illinois, USA; Christine Aguila, John Lanier, Armando Mata, and Ellen Sellergren from **Lakeview Learning Center**, Chicago, Illinois, USA; Ellen Gomez from **Laney College**, Oakland, California, USA; Brian White from **Northeastern Illinois University**, Chicago, Illinois, USA; Randi Reppen from **Northern Arizona University**, Flagstaff, Arizona, USA; Janine Gluud from **San Francisco State University – College of Extended Learning**, San Francisco, California, USA; Peg Sarosy from **San Francisco State University – American Language Institute**, San Francisco, California, USA; David Mitchell from **UC Berkley Extension, ELP – English Language Program**, San Francisco, California, USA; Eileen Censotti, Kim Knutson, Dave Onufrock, Marnie Ramker, and Jerry Stanfield from **University of Illinois at Chicago – Tutorium in Intensive English**, Chicago, Illinois, USA; Johnnie Johnson Hafernik from **University of San Francisco, ESL Program**, San Francisco, California, USA; Judy Friedman from **New York Institute of Technology**, New York, New York, USA; Sheila Hackner from **St. John's University**, New York, New York, USA; Joan Lesikin from **William Paterson University**, Wayne, New Jersey, USA; Linda Pelc from **LaGuardia Community College**, Long Island City, New York, USA; Tamara Plotnick from **Pace University**, New York, USA; Lenore Rosenbluth from **Montclair State University**, Montclair, New Jersey, USA; Suzanne Seidel from **Nassau Community College**, Garden City, New York, USA; Debbie Un from **New York University, New School**, and **LaGuardia Community College**, New York, New York, USA; Cynthia Wiseman from **Hunter College**, New York, New York, USA; Aaron Lawson from **Cornell University**, Ithaca, New York, USA, for his help in corpus research; Belkis Yanes from **CTC Belo Monte**, Caracas, Venezuela; Victoria García from **English World**, Caracas, Venezuela; Kevin Bandy from **LT Language Teaching Services**, Caracas, Venezuela; Ivonne Quintero from **PDVSA**, Caracas, Venezuela.

Piloters:

Daniela Jorge from **ELFE Idiomas**, São Paulo, Brazil; Eloisa Marchesi Oliveira from **ETE Professor Camargo Aranha**, São Paulo, Brazil; Marilena Wanderley Pessoa from **IBEU**, Rio de Janeiro, Brazil; Marcia Lotaif from **LTC**, São Paulo, Brazil; Mirlei Valenzi from **USP English on Campus**, São Paulo, Brazil; Jelena Johanovic from **YEP International**, São Paulo, Brazil; James Steinman from **Osaka International College for Women**, Moriguchi, Japan; Brad Visgatis from **Osaka International University for Women**, Moriguchi, Japan; William Figoni from **Osaka Institute of Technology**, Osaka, Japan; Terry O'Brien from **Otani Women's University**, Tondabayashi, Japan; Gregory Kennerly from **YMCA Language Center** piloted at **Hankyu SHS**, Osaka, Japan; Daniel Alejandro Ramos and Salvador Enríquez Castaneda from **Instituto Cultural Mexicano-Norteamericano de Jalisco**, Guadalajara, Mexico; Patricia Robinson and Melida Valdes from **Universidad de Guadalajara**, Guadalajara, Mexico.

We would also like to thank the people who arranged recordings:

Debbie Berktold, Bobbie Gore, Bill Kohler, Aaron Lawson, Terri Massin, Traci Suiter, Bryan Swan, and the many people who agreed to be recorded.

The authors would like to thank the **editorial** and **production** team: Sue Aldcorn, Janet Battiste, Sylvia P. Bloch, David Bohlke, Karen Brock, Jeff Chen, Sarah A. Cole, Sylvia Dare, Karen Davy, Jane Evison, Jill Freshney, Deborah Goldblatt, Paul Heacock, Louisa Hellegers, Cindee Howard, Eliza Jensen, Lesley Koustaff, Heather McCarron, Lise R. Minovitz, Diana Nam, Kathy Niemczyk, Sandra Pike, Danielle Power, Bill Preston, Janet Raskin, Mary Sandre, Tamar Savir, Susannah Sodergren, Shelagh Speers, Kayo Taguchi, Mary Vaughn, Jennifer Wilkin, Dorothy E. Zemach, and all the design and production team at Adventure House.

And these Cambridge University Press **staff** and **advisors**: Yumiko Akeba, Jim Anderson, Kanako Aoki, Mary Louise Baez, Carlos Barbisan, Alexandre Canizares, Cruz Castro, Kathleen Corley, Kate Cory-Wright, Riitta da Costa, Peter Davison, Elizabeth Fuzikava, Steven Golden, Yuri Hara, Catherine Higham, Gareth Knight, João Madureira, Andy Martin, Alejandro Martínez, Nigel McQuitty, Carine Mitchell, Mark O'Neil, Rebecca Ou, Antonio Puente, Colin Reublinger, Andrew Robinson, Dan Schulte, Kumiko Sekioka, Catherine Shih, Howard Siegelman, Ivan Sorrentino, Ian Sutherland, Alcione Tavares, Koen Van Landeghem, Sergio Varela, and Ellen Zlotnick.

In addition, the authors would like to thank Colin Hayes and Jeremy Mynott for making the project possible in the first place. Most of all, very special thanks are due to Mary Vaughn for her dedication, support, and professionalism. Helen Sandiford would like to thank her family and especially her husband, Bryan Swan, for his support and love.

Welcome to Touchstone!

We created the ***Touchstone*** series with the help of the *Cambridge International Corpus* of North American English. The corpus is a large database of language from everyday conversations, radio and television broadcasts, and newspapers and books.

Using computer software, we analyze the corpus to find out how people actually use English. We use the corpus as a "touchstone" to make sure that each lesson teaches you authentic and useful language. The corpus helps us choose and explain the grammar, vocabulary, and conversation strategies you need to communicate successfully in English.

Touchstone makes learning English fun. It gives you many different opportunities to interact with your classmates. You can exchange personal information, take class surveys, role-play situations, play games, and discuss topics of personal interest. Using ***Touchstone***, you can develop confidence in your ability to understand real-life English and to express yourself clearly and effectively in everyday situations.

We hope you enjoy using ***Touchstone*** and wish you every success with your English classes.

Michael McCarthy
Jeanne McCarten
Helen Sandiford

Unit features

Getting started *presents new grammar in natural contexts such as articles, surveys, interviews, conversations, and anecdotes.*

Figure it out *challenges you to notice how grammar works.*

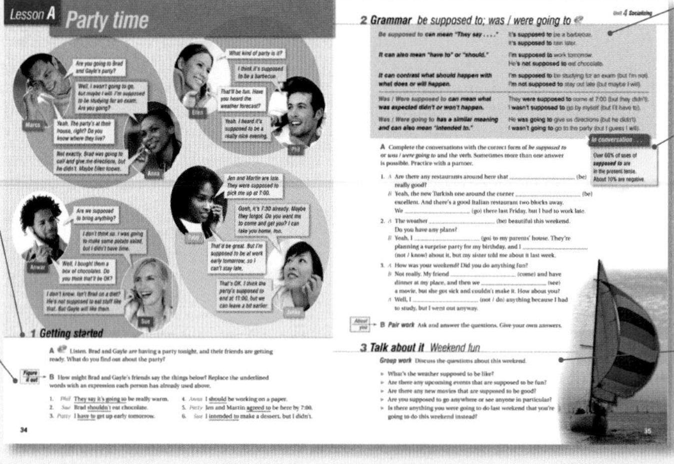
Lesson A Party time
1 Getting started
2 Grammar be supposed to; was / were going to
3 Talk about it Weekend fun

Grammar *is presented in clear charts.*

In conversation *panels tell you about the grammar and vocabulary that are most frequent in spoken North American English.*

Talk about it *encourages yo to discuss interesting questio with your classmates.*

Building vocabulary and grammar *combines new vocabulary and structures in one presentation, often to teach the grammar of a particular vocabulary set. In some units, vocabulary and grammar are presented separately.*

Word sort *helps you organize vocabulary and then use it to interact with your classmates.*

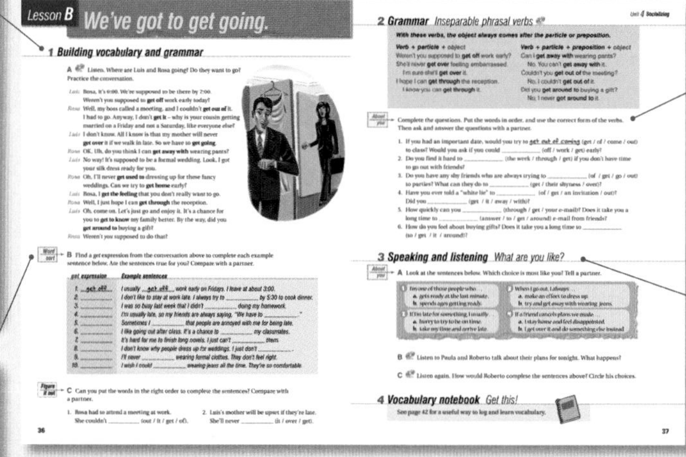
Lesson B We've got to get going.
1 Building vocabulary and grammar
2 Grammar Inseparable phrasal verbs
3 Speaking and listening What are you like?
4 Vocabulary notebook Get this!

Grammar exercises *give yc practice with new structures and opportunities to exchang personal information with you classmates.*

Speaking and listening *ski are often practiced together. You listen to a variety of conversations based on real-li language. Tasks include "liste and react" activities.*

:onversation strategy
·elps you "manage"
·onversations better. In this
·sson, you learn how to
·heck your understanding
·y asking questions in the
·rm of statements. The
trategies are based on
·xamples from the corpus.

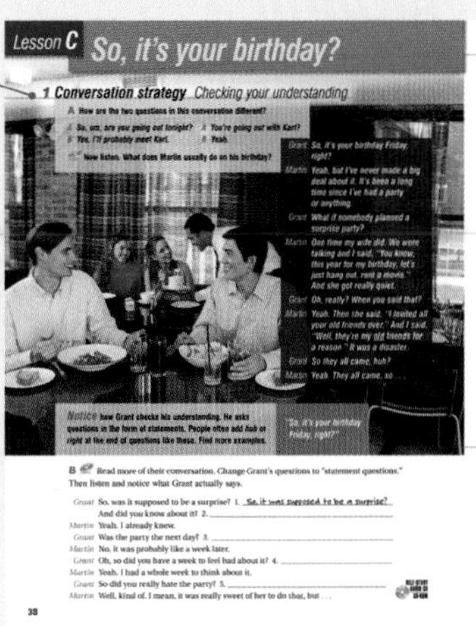

2 Strategy plus so

3 Speaking naturally Being sure or checking

Strategy plus teaches important words and expressions for conversation management, such as using **so** to start or close a topic.

Speaking naturally helps you understand and use natural pronunciation and intonation.

eading has interesting
·exts from newspapers,
·nagazines, interviews, and
·he Internet. The activities
·elp you develop reading
·kills.

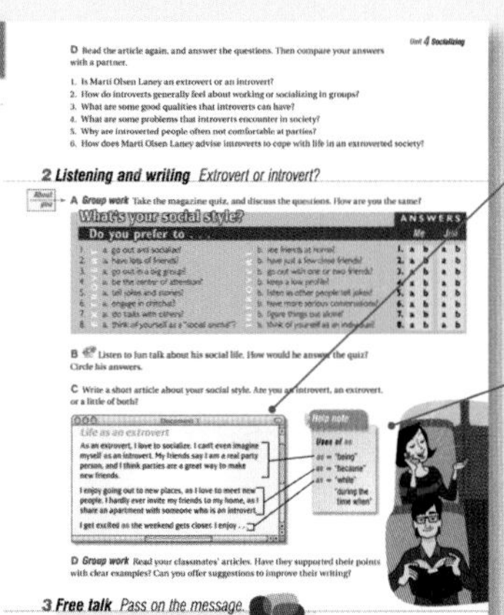

Writing tasks include stories, interview questions, letters, short articles, and proposals.

Help notes give you information on things like punctuation, linking ideas, and organizing information.

ocabulary notebook is
· page of fun activities to
·elp you organize and write
·own vocabulary.

ord builder activities
·ive you extra words and
·xpressions to research
·nd learn, allowing you to
·xtend your vocabulary
·ven more.

n your own is a practical
·ask to help you learn
·ocabulary outside of class.

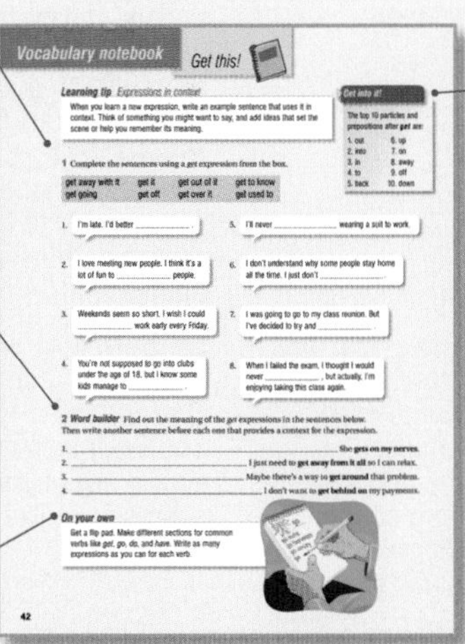

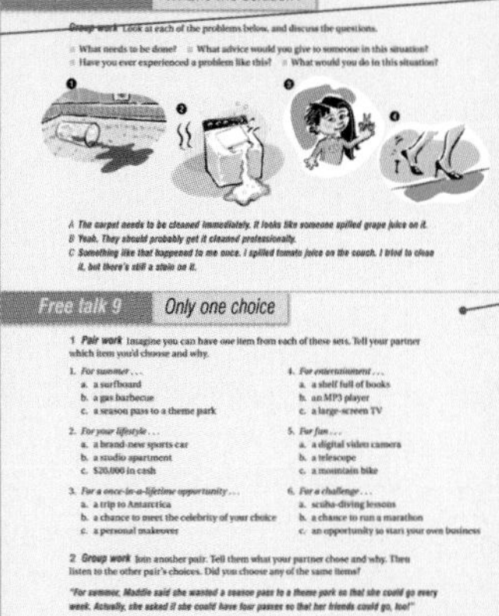

Fun facts from the corpus tell you the most frequent words and expressions for different topics.

Free talk helps you engage in free conversation with your classmates.

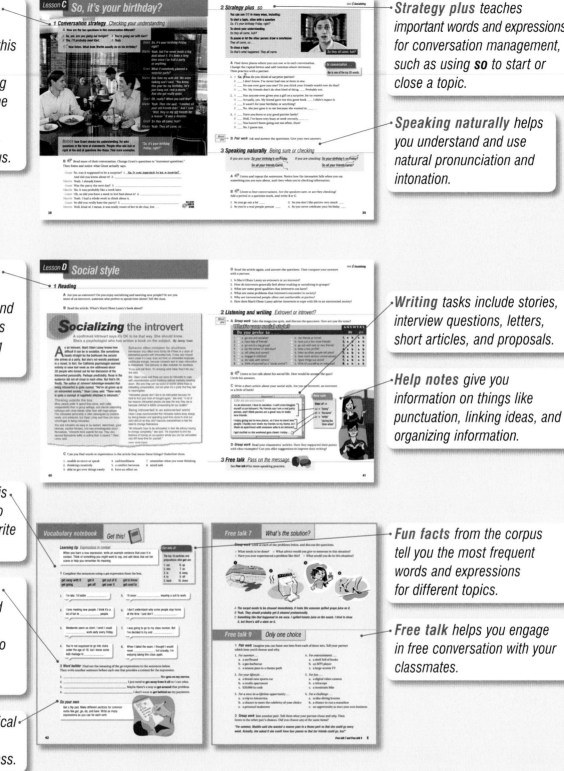

ther features

· ***Touchstone checkpoint*** ·fter every three units ·eviews grammar, ·ocabulary, and ·onversation strategies.

A ***Self-study Audio CD/ CD-ROM*** gives you more practice with listening, speaking, and vocabulary building.

The ***Class Audio Program*** presents the conversations and listening activities in natural, lively English.

The ***Workbook*** gives you language practice and extra reading and writing activities. ***Progress checks*** help you assess your progress.

Touchstone Level 4A Scope and sequence

	Functions / Topics	Grammar	Vocabulary	Conversation strategies	Pronunciation
Unit 1 **Interesting lives** *pages 1–10*	▪ Ask questions to find out about someone's interests and background ▪ Tell interesting stories about your own life	▪ Review of simple and continuous forms of verbs ▪ Verbs followed by verb + *-ing* or *to* + verb	▪ Verbs followed by verb + *-ing* or *to* + verb	▪ Use the present tense to highlight key moments in a story ▪ Use *this* and *these* to highlight important people, things, and events in a story	▪ Reductions of auxiliary verbs and the pronoun *you* in questions
Unit 2 **Personal tastes** *pages 11–20*	▪ Talk about makeovers, style, and fashion ▪ Talk about your tastes in clothes and music	▪ Make comparisons with *as . . . as* and *not as . . . as* ▪ Ask negative questions when you want or expect someone to agree with you	▪ Colors, patterns, materials, and styles of clothing	▪ Show understanding by summarizing what people say ▪ Use *Now* to introduce a follow-up question on a different aspect of a topic	▪ Linking words with the same consonant sound
Unit 3 **World cultures** *pages 21–30*	▪ Talk about aspects of your culture ▪ Talk about manners, customs, and culturally appropriate behavior	▪ The simple present passive ▪ Verb + *-ing* as a subject and after prepositions ▪ *to* + verb after *It's . . .* ▪ Position of *not*	▪ Cultural items, icons, and events ▪ Manners, customs, and culturally appropriate behavior	▪ Use expressions like *in fact* to sound more direct when you speak ▪ Use *of course* to give information that is not surprising, or to show you understand or agree	▪ Silent syllables in which unstressed vowels are not pronounced
			Touchstone **checkpoint Units 1–3**	**pages 31–32**	

	Functions / Topics	Grammar	Vocabulary	Conversation strategies	Pronunciation
Unit 4 **Socializing** *pages 33–42*	▪ Talk about things you are supposed to do, things you were supposed to do, and things that are supposed to happen ▪ Talk about going out and socializing	▪ *be supposed to, was / were supposed to,* and *was / were going to* ▪ Inseparable phrasal verbs	▪ Expressions with *get*	▪ Check your understanding by using questions in the form of statements ▪ Use *so* to start or close a topic, to check your understanding, to pause, or to let someone draw a conclusion	▪ Intonation of sentences when you are sure vs. when you are checking
Unit 5 **Law and order** *pages 43–52*	▪ Talk about rules and regulations ▪ Talk about crime and punishment	▪ The passive of modal verbs ▪ *get* passive vs. *be* passive ▪ *catch* + verb + *-ing*	▪ Rules and regulations ▪ Crimes and offenses, the people who commit them, and punishments	▪ Organize your views with expressions like *First (of all)* ▪ Show someone has a valid argument with expressions like *That's a good point*	▪ Saying conversational expressions
Unit 6 **Strange events** *pages 53–62*	▪ Talk about coincidences and strange events ▪ Talk about belief in superstitions	▪ The past perfect ▪ Responses with *So* and *Neither*	▪ Strange events ▪ Superstitions from around the world	▪ Repeat your ideas in another way to make your meaning clear ▪ Use *just* to make your meaning stronger or softer	▪ Stressing new information
			Touchstone **checkpoint Units 4–6**	**pages 63–64**	

Listening	Reading	Writing	Vocabulary notebook	Free talk
A lucky escape ▪ Listen for details in a story, and retell it with a partner; then role-play a conversation about it *Facing a challenge* ▪ Listen to a true story, and answer questions	*My story: Pat Galloway* ▪ A magazine article about a successful engineer and the story of how she chose her profession	▪ Write a story about a time in your life when you faced a challenge ▪ Format for writing an anecdote or a story	*Mottoes* ▪ Write down the verb forms that can follow new verbs, and use them in sentences	*An interview with . . .* ▪ Pair work: Complete interesting questions to ask a classmate; then interview each other, and note your partner's answers
My music collection ▪ Listen for details in a conversation, and answer questions; then listen and choose the best responses *What's your thing?* ▪ Listen to four people talk about their tastes, and identify the topics they discuss; then listen and answer questions	*A free spirit!* ▪ An interview with a woman with very individual tastes	▪ Write questions to interview a partner on his or her personal style; write answers to your partner's questions ▪ Punctuation review: comma, dash, and exclamation mark	*Blue suede shoes* ▪ Find and label pictures that illustrate new words	*What's popular?* ▪ Group work: Discuss questions about current popular tastes and how tastes have changed
Away from home ▪ Listen to a woman talk about being away from home, and answer questions as she would *Favorite proverbs* ▪ Listen to four people talk about proverbs, and number them; then match them with English equivalents, and listen to check	*Counting Chickens* ▪ A magazine article about the use and misuse of proverbs	▪ Write an article about your favorite proverb and how it relates to your life ▪ Useful expressions for writing about proverbs or sayings	*Travel etiquette* ▪ Find examples of new words and expressions you have learned in magazines, in newspapers, and on the Internet	*Local customs* ▪ Pair work: Prepare a presentation on local customs for visitors to your country, and then present it to the class

Touchstone checkpoint Units 1–3 pages 31–32

What are you like? ▪ Listen to people talk about plans, and summarize them; then listen and complete sentences as the man would *Extrovert or introvert?* ▪ Take a quiz; then listen to a man talk about his social style, and answer the quiz as he would	*Socializing the introvert* ▪ A magazine article about a book on introverts living in an extroverted society	▪ Write an article about your own social style as an extrovert, an introvert, or a little of both ▪ Uses of *as*	*Get this!* ▪ Learn new expressions by writing example sentences that use them in context	*Pass on the message.* ▪ Class activity: Play a game where you pass a message to a classmate through another classmate, and then listen to see if your message is delivered correctly
We got robbed! ▪ Listen to a conversation, and answer questions; then listen and choose true sentences *Different points of view* ▪ Listen to a debate, and answer questions; then listen and respond to different points of view	*Cam phones, go home!* ▪ A magazine article about the cam-phone craze	▪ Write a letter to the editor of a magazine, responding to the article on cam phones ▪ Give reasons with *because*, *since*, and *as*	*It's a crime!* ▪ Write down new words in word charts that group related ideas together by topic	*Lawmakers* ▪ Pair work: Choose a topic and debate the pros and cons of three possible new laws; then join another pair with the same topic, and compare arguments
It's a small world! ▪ Listen to a woman tell a story, and answer questions *Lucky or not?* ▪ Listen to four people talk about superstitions, and determine if the things they are about are lucky or unlucky; then listen and write down each superstition	*Separated at birth . . .* ▪ A magazine article about the true story of twins who found each other after growing up in different adoptive families	▪ Write a true story from your own family history ▪ Prepositional time clauses	*Keep your fingers crossed.* ▪ Use word webs to group new sayings or superstitions by topic	*Can you believe it?* ▪ Pair work: Take turns telling each other true stories about unusual beliefs and strange events in your life

Touchstone checkpoint Units 4–6 pages 63–64

Working in groups

We're ready now, aren't we?

Are we ready? Let's get started.

Haven't I interviewed you already?

I've already interviewed you, haven't I?

Where are we?

We're on number ________ .

We haven't quite finished yet.

Neither have we.

We still need more time – just a few more minutes.

So do we.

One interesting thing we found out was that ________ .

________ told us that ________________ .

Checking with the teacher

Would it be OK if I missed our class tomorro
I have to ________ .

I'm sorry I missed the last class. What do I need to do to catch up?

When are we supposed to hand in our homewor

Excuse me. My homework needs to be checked.

I'm sorry. I haven't finished my homework.
I was going to do it last night, but ________

Will we be reviewing this before the next test?

"______" means "______," doesn't it?
It's a regular verb, isn't it?

I'm not sure I understand what we're supposed to
Could you explain the activity again, please?

Could I please be excused? I'll be right bac

Unit 1

eresting lives

1, you learn how to . . .

e and continuous forms of verbs (review).
that are followed by verb + *-ing* or *to* + verb.
eresting story about your life.
esent tense to highlight key moments

nd *these* to highlight important people,
d events.

Before you begin . . .

Do you know any interesting people?
Why do you think they are interesting?
What interesting things do they do?

Interviews

English Department Newsletter

You should really get to know **Melida Cortez**, a graduate student in our English Department. Also a talented artist, she spends her free time painting, and she started a sculpture class last month. She hopes one day to have an exhibition of her work.

Student of the month – Melida Cortez

How long have you been living here?
I've been living in Mexico City for five years. I came here to go to school originally. It's a great place to live.

Have you ever lived in another country?
No, I haven't. But my brother has. He's been living in Bogotá, in Colombia, for almost a year now. I'm going to visit him later this year.

What kind of music are you listening to currently?
Well, of course I love Latin music. I'm listening to a lot of Latin jazz right now. I like to listen to music when I paint.

What's your favorite way of spending an evening? What do you do?
I like to go out with my friends – we go and eat someplace, and then go dancing all night!

When did you last buy yourself a treat?
Last week, actually. I was at a friend's art studio, and I fell in love with one of her paintings. So I bought it.

What did you do for your last birthday?
I went home and had a big party with my family.

What's the nicest thing anyone has ever done for you?
Actually, about six months ago, I was complaining to my dad that I didn't know how to drive, so he paid for some driving lessons. I was thrilled.

Who or what is the greatest love of your life?
Oh, chocolate! I can't get through the day without some.

What were you doing at this time yesterday?
I was sitting on a bus. We were stuck in traffic for an hour!

1 Getting started

A Read the interview with Melida. Do you have anything in common with her? Tell the class.

B Can you choose the correct form of each question? Circle ***a*** or ***b***. Use the interview above to help you. Then ask and answer the questions with a partner.

1. a. What book do you read currently? b. What book are you reading currently?
2. a. When did you last see a really good movie? b. When were you last seeing a really good movi
3. a. Have you ever stayed up all night? b. Have you ever been staying up all night?

2 Grammar *Simple and continuous verbs (review)*

Simple verbs: for completed actions or permanent situations	***Continuous verbs: for ongoing actions or temporary situations***
What kind of music **do** you **listen** to? I **love** Latin music. I **listen** to it a lot.	What kind of music **are** you **listening** to currently? I**'m listening** to a lot of Latin jazz right now.
Have you ever **lived** in another country? No, I**'ve** never **lived** anywhere else.	How long **have** you **been living** here? I**'ve been living** here for five years.
What **did** you **do** for your last birthday? I **went** home and **had** a big party.	What **were** you **doing** at this time yesterday? I **was sitting** on a bus.

A Complete the questions and answers. Use the simple or continuous form of the verb in the present, past, or present perfect. Then practice with a partner.

1. *A* Who __do__ you ____admire____ (admire) the most?
   B I ____________ (admire) my grandfather. He ____________ (teach) me a lot when I ____________ (grow up).
2. *A* ________ you ever ________ (meet) anyone famous?
   B No, but last year, I ____________ (see) a TV star on the street. We ______ both ____________ (wait) in line for ice cream.
3. *A* When ________ you last ________ (get) a good workout?
   B Yesterday. In fact, I ____________ (lift) weights when you ____________ (call) me last night.
4. *A* What ________ you ________ (do) for a living?
   B Actually, I ____________ (not work) right now. I ____________ (look) for a job for six months, but I ____________ (not find) anything yet.
5. *A* What ________ you ________ (do) for fun lately?
   B Not much. I ____________ (work) really hard for the past year. In fact, I ____________ (not take) a vacation in over a year now.

About you → **B** ***Pair work*** Ask and answer the questions. Give your own answers.

3 Speaking naturally *Reductions in questions*

*How long **have you** been learning English?*
*What **do you** like to do in your English class?*
*Why **are you** learning English?*
*What **did you** do in your last class?*

A Listen and repeat the questions. Notice the reductions of the auxiliary verbs and the pronoun *you*. Then ask and answer the questions with a partner.

About you → **B** ***Pair work*** Take turns asking the questions in the interview on page 2. Pay attention to your pronunciation of the auxiliary verbs and the pronoun *you*.

Lesson B It's a long story!

1 Building vocabulary and grammar

A Listen to Dan's story. Answer the questions.

1. Where did Dan live before he moved to Seoul?
2. Why did he want to go to South Korea?
3. How did he get his job there?
4. What did his new company offer him?

Living abroad: Dan's story

Dan Anderson was born in the U.S.A. He's now living in South Korea. We asked him, "How did you **end up** living in Seoul?"

Dan: Well, it's a long story! Before I came here, I **spent** three years working for a small company in Tokyo while I **finished** doing my master's in business. To be honest, I wasn't **planning on** leaving or anything. But one day, I **happened** to be in the office, and one of the salesmen was reading the newspaper.

He knew I was **considering** going to South Korea someday – you see, my mother's Korean, and I've always been interested in the culture and everything – and anyway, he leaned over and said, "Dan, this **seems** to be the perfect job for you. Check this out."

I looked at the ad, and I **remember** thinking, "Should I **bother** to apply?" But I **decided** to go for it even though I didn't **expect** to get it, and to make a long story short, I got the job!

The company **offered** to transfer me to Seoul, and they **agreed** to pay for my Korean lessons. I **started** working here two months later. And the rest is history.

I mean, I **miss** living in Japan, but you can't have it both ways, I guess. Actually, I can't **imagine** living anywhere else now!

Word sort → **B** Can you sort the verbs in bold above into the correct categories? Which verbs are followed by verb + *-ing*? Which are followed by *to* + verb?

Verbs followed by verb + -ing	
end up (living)	
spend (3 years working)	

Verbs followed by to + verb	
happen (to be)	

2 Grammar *Verb complements: verb + -ing or to + verb*

Verb + verb + -ing:** consider finish imagine miss mind spend **(time)	He **finished reading** his newspaper. I **spent** three years **working** in Tokyo.
***Verb + particle / preposition + verb + -ing:** end up keep on think about plan on*	How did you **end up living** here? I wasn't **planning on leaving** Japan.
***Verb + to + verb:** agree decide happen offer seem intend expect*	They **agreed to pay** for Korean lessons. I didn't **expect to get** the job.
***Verb + -ing or to + verb with a different meaning:** remember stop try*	I **stopped talking** to him. I **stopped to talk** to him.
***Verb + -ing or to + verb with the same meaning:** begin bother continue start like love hate*	Should I **bother applying**? Should I **bother to apply**?

Complete the conversations with the correct forms of the verbs given. Then practice with a partner.

1. *A* How did you end up studying (study) here?
   B My friend recommended this school, so I decided ________ (sign up) for this class. How about you?
   A Well, I wasn't planning on ________ (learn) English, but my company offered ________ (pay) for my classes. I agreed ________ (come), and here I am! I want to keep on ________ (take) classes if I can.
2. *A* How did you get your current job?
   B It's a long story! I started ________ (work) there as an assistant, and I spent months just ________ (file) papers. I didn't mind ________ (do) that for a while, but then I happened ________ (hear) about a new sales position. I never intended ________ (be) a sales rep, but now I can't imagine ________ (do) anything else.

In conversation . . .

***Begin**, **bother**, **continue**, **like**, **love**, and **hate** are followed more often by **to** + **verb**. **Start** is followed more often by **verb** + **-ing**.*

3 Talk about it *How did you end up doing that?*

Group work Has anyone in your group done these things? Find out the whole story. Ask the follow-up questions below, and add more questions of your own.

Who . . .	Then ask:
▶ has taken an interesting class?	What made you decide to do that?
▶ used to have an unusual job?	How did you end up working there?
▶ has met a celebrity?	Were you expecting to meet him or her?
▶ has taken an exotic trip?	Are you planning on going again?
▶ used to have a bad habit?	What made you stop doing that?
▶ has done something scary?	Would you ever consider doing that again?

4 Vocabulary notebook *Mottoes*

See page 10 for a new way to log and learn vocabulary.

Lesson C We're both getting scared. . . .

1 Conversation strategy *Highlighting key moments in a story*

A Juan is telling his friend Kim a story. Underline the verbs in his sentences below. What tenses does he use?

Juan ***We were on this trail, and it was getting dark. Then Bryan says, "Where are we?"***

Now listen to Juan and Bryan tell Kim the whole story. What happened to them?

Juan **Remember that time we were hiking in Utah?**
Bryan **When we got lost? That was funny.**
Kim **Why? What happened?**
Juan **We were on this trail, and it was getting dark. Then Bryan says, "Where are we?"**
Bryan **Yeah, we couldn't see a thing, and we walked off the trail. It was that bad.**
Juan **Yeah, there were all these trees around us, and we were so lost. And we're thinking, "Oh, no." And we're both getting kind of scared. We just wanted to get out of there.**
Kim **I bet.**
Juan **And Bryan says, "Should we jog a little?" And I go, "Yeah. I was thinking the same thing. Let's go."**
Bryan **So we started jogging, . . .**
Juan **And we said to each other, "We've got to stick together, in case anything happens."**

Notice **how Juan changes to the present tense at key moments in his story. It makes them more "dramatic." Find examples in the conversation.**

"We're both getting kind of scared."

B Read more of their conversation. Change the underlined verbs to the simple present or present continuous to make the story more dramatic. Then listen and check your answers.

Bryan Yeah. And all of a sudden, we heard this noise.
Juan And I looked over at Bryan, and I saw his face was white, and he was starting to run fast.
Bryan Well, yeah. I mean, it was a weird noise.
Juan So, I was thinking, "Wait a minute. What happened to our plan to stick together?" So I started to run with him.
Bryan Yeah, we were running through the trees, scared to death. It was hilarious! It was just like in a movie.

2 Strategy plus *this and these in stories*

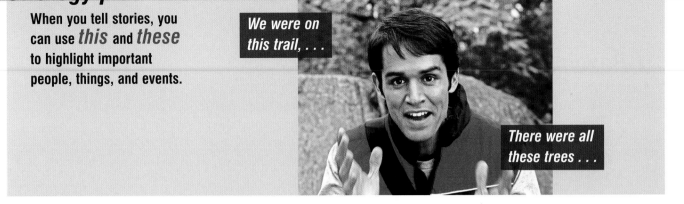

When you tell stories, you can use *this* and *these* to highlight important people, things, and events.

We were on this trail, . . .
There were all these trees . . .

A ***Pair work*** Replace *a, an,* and *some* with *this* or *these* in the stories below. Then take turns telling the stories.

1. "I have **an** aunt who's really into old paintings – she's always buying them at junk shops and yard sales. And in every room in her house, she has **some** old pictures on all the walls. Well, one time she goes to **a** yard sale, sees **a** picture, and buys it for practically nothing. And guess what? It turned out to be worth thousands!"
2. "I have **a** friend who's always getting into funny situations. One time she was invited to **a** party, and she got totally lost. Anyway, she sees **a** house with **some** cars parked in front of it, and she thought it was the right place. So she knocks on the door, and **a** nice guy lets her in. She had dinner there and everything before she realized it was the wrong party!"

About you

B ***Pair work*** Tell one of the stories above from memory, or tell an interesting story of your own. Remember to use *this* or *these* to highlight important people, things, and events.

3 Listening and speaking *A lucky escape*

A You're going to hear Aaron tell a story about a skiing accident. He was skiing with some friends when one of them fell down the mountain. Circle four questions you want to ask Aaron.

1. Where were you skiing?
2. How far did your friend fall?
3. What did you do when he fell?
4. How badly was he hurt?
5. Did you get help? How?
6. Did he have to go to the hospital?
7. When did this happen?
8. Is he OK now?

B Listen. Write answers to the questions you chose. Then share answers with a partner. Can you remember the story together? Consult other classmates if necessary.

C ***Pair work*** Role-play a conversation about the accident. Take turns telling the story and asking the questions.

Against the odds

1 Reading

A Think of someone you know who has become very successful. In what way is this person successful? Did he or she face any challenges along the way? Tell the class.

B Read the article. What profession did Pat Galloway choose? What did she like about it?

My story: Pat Galloway

"Bad idea. You'll flunk out."

A successful engineer tells her story.

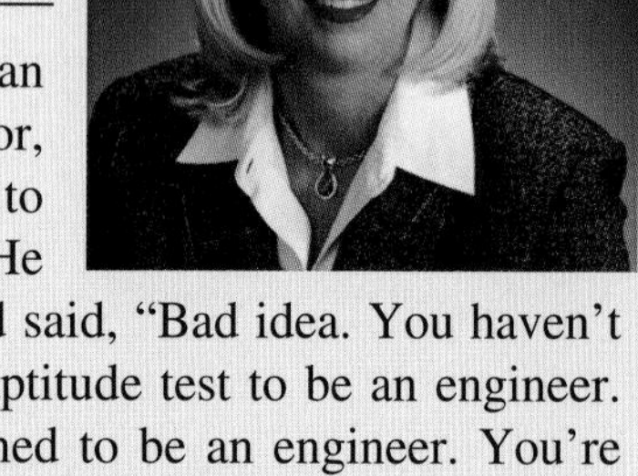

When I was in high school in Kentucky in 1974, I was into the arts. I was a dancer, in the drama club, on the debate team. I was an artist. I had no chemistry, no physics, and no calculus at all. But one day at a required high school lecture, a civil-engineering professor from the University of Kentucky arrived to speak, showing all these renderings of buildings. I was fascinated with the fact that I might be able to draw and get paid for it. And according to him, I could improve the quality of life for people and be a problem solver. Well, I became so excited, I went home and told my mother, a teacher, that I wanted to be a civil engineer. My mother had a motto that I have followed to this day: "If you really want to do something, you put your mind to it. Don't ever let anyone tell you it can't be done." So when I told her, she said, "Great."

Then reality hit when I went back to my guidance counselor the next day and told him that instead of being a lawyer or an interior decorator, I now wanted to be an engineer. He looked at me and said, "Bad idea. You haven't scored on your aptitude test to be an engineer. You're not inclined to be an engineer. You're not made up to be an engineer." Then I went to my math teacher, and she said the same thing, "Bad idea. You'll flunk out."

I went to my grandmother, and her reaction was, "Isn't that a man's job?" And that's what really solidified it. I had two people tell me I wasn't intelligent enough, which I couldn't understand because I was a straight-A student, and now I had someone else tell me that it was a man's job. So I was bound and determined to prove everyone wrong. And I did. In 1978, I graduated from Purdue University in three years with a B+ average and a degree in civil engineering.

– as told to Deirdre van Dyk

C What do these words and expressions from the article mean? Choose ***a*** or ***b***. How did you guess the meaning? Tell a partner.

1. you'll flunk out	a. you'll fail and leave college	b. you'll graduate
2. renderings	a. photographs	b. drawings
3. according to him	a. he said	b. I said
4. a motto	a. a promise	b. a rule to live by
5. put your mind to it	a. forget about it	b. try hard to do it
6. you're not inclined to be	a. you're not the type to be	b. you're not afraid to be
7. solidified it	a. convinced me	b. worried me
8. I was bound and determined	a. I was very angry	b. I was very focused

D Read the article again. Are the sentences true or false? Correct the false sentences.

	True	False
1. *Pat always planned on being a civil engineer.*	☐	☐
2. *She first became interested in engineering because she loved math and science.*	☐	☐
3. *Her mother encouraged her to follow her dream.*	☐	☐
4. *Pat's teachers expected her to be in a profession like engineering.*	☐	☐
5. *Pat wanted to prove to everyone that she could be a civil engineer.*	☐	☐
6. *Pat refused to let any problems stop her along the way.*	☐	☐

2 Listening and writing *Facing a challenge*

A Listen to a true story about Lance Armstrong. Complete the sentences with the correct information. Choose ***a***, ***b***, or ***c***.

1. As a teenager, Lance Armstrong became a professional ______________ .
   a. swimmer　b. cyclist　c. triathlete
2. He says he got his ambition from his ______________ .
   a. close friend　b. mother　c. high school teacher
3. He is now ______________ athlete.
   a. an amateur　b. a professional　c. a retired
4. The biggest challenge he faced was ______________ .
   a. a serious illness　b. the media　c. losing races
5. He has won more ______________ than anyone else.
   a. cycling races　b. Olympic medals　c. Tour de France races

B Think about a time in your life when you had to do something difficult. What did you have to do? How did you feel? How did you feel afterwards? Write a story about that time.

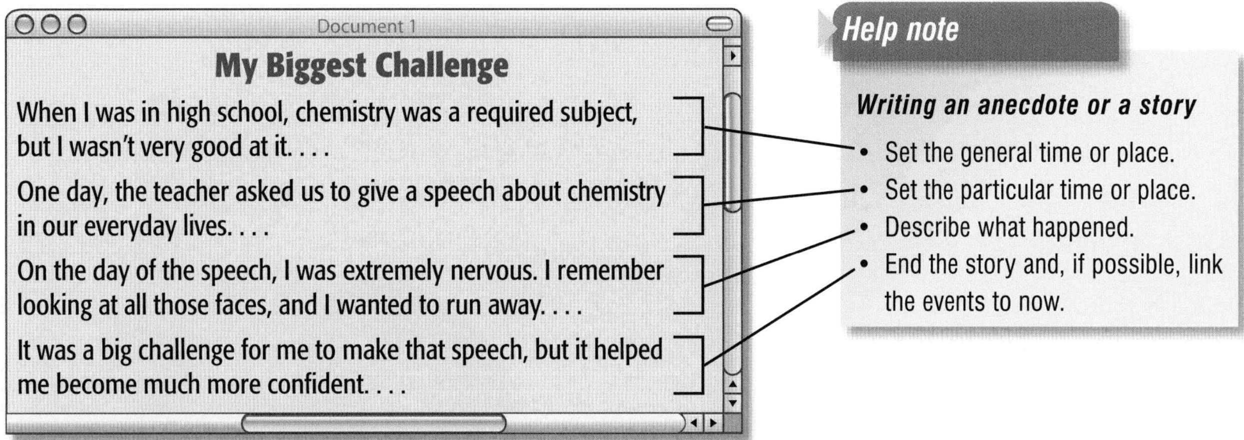
Document 1

My Biggest Challenge

When I was in high school, chemistry was a required subject, but I wasn't very good at it. . . .

One day, the teacher asked us to give a speech about chemistry in our everyday lives. . . .

On the day of the speech, I was extremely nervous. I remember looking at all those faces, and I wanted to run away. . . .

It was a big challenge for me to make that speech, but it helped me become much more confident. . . .

Help note

Writing an anecdote or a story

- Set the general time or place.
- Set the particular time or place.
- Describe what happened.
- End the story and, if possible, link the events to now.

C ***Pair work*** Read a partner's story. Then ask questions to find out more about the story.

3 Free talk *An interview with . . .*

See ***Free talk 1*** at the back of the book for more speaking practice.

Vocabulary notebook

Mottoes

Learning tip Verb patterns

When you learn a new verb, write down the verb form(s) that can follow it. Then use it in a sentence. For example:

imagine verb + -ing	I can't imagine having lots of money.
decide to + verb	I've decided to be a doctor.
start verb + -ing	I'm going to start saving money.
start to + verb	I'm going to start to save money.

1 Write down the form(s) of the verbs that can follow the verbs below. Then complete the mottoes. Use the correct form(s) of the verbs given.

1. agree to + verb "Never agree ________ (lend) money to strangers."
2. intend ________ "If you don't intend ________ (do) something properly,
   bother ________ don't bother ________ (start) it!"
3. stop ________ "Never stop ________ (do) the things you
   enjoy ________ enjoy ________ (do)."
4. keep on ________ "Keep on ________ (try) until you find success."
5. consider ________ "Consider ________ (take) every opportunity you get in life."
6. seem ________ "Things aren't always what they seem ________ (be)."

2 ***Word builder*** Find out the meanings of these verbs, and write down the verb form(s) that can follow them. Then make up your own motto for each verb.

1. give up ________ ________________
2. promise ________ ________________
3. put off ________ ________________
4. refuse ________ ________________

On your own

Make a flip pad for the new verbs you have learned in this unit. Write each new verb in a sentence. Every time you have a spare minute, learn a verb!

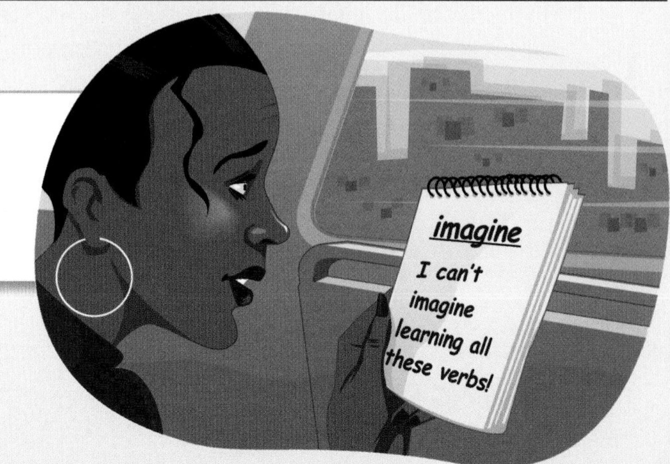

Unit 2

Personal tastes

In Unit 2, you learn how to . . .

- make comparisons with *(not) as . . . as*.
- ask negative questions when you want someone to agree.
- talk about fashion and your tastes in clothes and music.
- show understanding by summarizing what people say.
- use *Now* to introduce a follow-up question on a different aspect of a topic.

2

1

4

3

Before you begin . . .

What kind of . . .

- music do you like?
- car would you like?
- clothes do you wear?
- hairstyle suits you?

Do you and your classmates have similiar tastes?

Makeovers

Would you let a friend give YOU a makeover?

We gave Cindy and Ron, two very good friends, the chance to choose a new look for each other. How did they do? Here's the verdict!

What do you think about your new look, Cindy?

I love it! I don't usually wear these colors, but this dress is really nice. I like it. I wouldn't usually wear this much makeup – I try to get ready as quickly as I can in the morning – but it looks good. I'm really pleased.

Ron, you chose a completely different look for Cindy. How do you like it?

I like it a lot. I tried as hard as I could to find a style that suits her personality better. Her hair looks great. I mean, I don't usually like short hair as much as long hair, but it suits her, I think. And I like the dress on her. She looks great.

After

How do you like your new look, Ron?

Well, I kind of like it. I'm not used to wearing pants like these, but they're just as comfortable as my jeans. And Cindy made a good choice with the suede jacket. It's cool. Yeah, I don't look as scruffy as I did!

Cindy, do you like Ron's new look? He looks very different!

Yes, I really like it. He doesn't usually pay much attention to how he looks – not as much as he should! Actually, the pastel shirt I chose doesn't look as good on him as the bright colors he usually wears. I don't think I like pastels that much after all. But overall, he looks a lot better! I like his hair short like that.

After

1 Getting started

A Look at Cindy's and Ron's "before" and "after" pictures, and listen to their comments. What do they like about their makeovers? Do you agree with their comments?

B How do Cindy and Ron actually say these things? Find the sentences in the article above. Compare with a partner.

1. *Ron* These pants and my jeans are equally comfortable.
2. *Cindy* Bright colors look better on him than the pastel shirt I chose.
3. *Ron* I usually prefer long hair to short hair.
4. *Ron* I used to look scruffier.

2 Grammar *Comparisons with (not) as . . . as*

Adjectives	The pants are just **as comfortable as** my jeans. I don't look **as scruffy as** I did.
Nouns	She spends **as little time as** possible on her makeup. She doesn't wear **as many bright colors as** she should. He doesn't pay **as much attention** to his appearance **as** he should.
Adverbs	I tried **as hard as** I could to find the right style for her. I don't like short hair **as much as** long hair.

About you

A Answer these questions with your own opinions. Use *as . . . as* or *not as . . . as.*

1. Are older people just as interested in fashion as young people?
2. Do older people care as much about their appearance as young people?
3. Do men get haircuts as often as women do?
4. Do men spend as much money on themselves as women?
5. Are makeover shows as interesting as other reality shows on TV?
6. When you choose clothes, are looks as important as comfort?
7. Do you have as many clothes as you'd like? How about pairs of shoes?
8. Do you spend as little time as possible shopping for clothes?

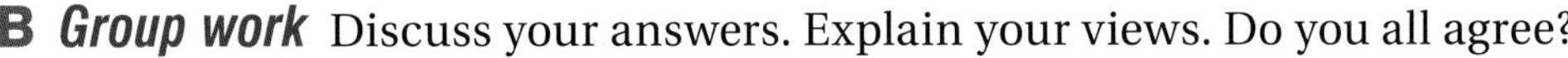

B *Group work* Discuss your answers. Explain your views. Do you all agree?

A ***It seems to me that older people are just as interested in fashion as young people.***
B ***I'm not sure. I don't think older people are as interested.***
C ***Well, my mother is a lot more interested in fashion than I am!***

3 Speaking naturally *Linking words with the same consonant sound*

big glasses *wear red* *dark colors* *some makeup* *stylish shoes*

A Listen and repeat the expressions above. Notice that when the same consonant sound is at the end of one word and at the start of the next, it is pronounced once, but it sounds longer.

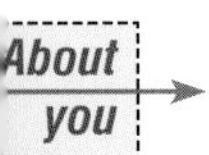

B Now listen and repeat these statements. Are they true for you? Discuss with a partner.

1. I don't like bi**g g**lasses. They're le**ss s**tylish than small glasses.
2. I think people loo**k c**ool in sunglasses.
3. I li**ke c**asual clothes. I can't stan**d d**ressing up for special occasions.
4. I think women should always wear so**me m**akeup.
5. I own a lot of bla**ck c**lothes. I ha**te t**o wear bright colors, and I never wea**r r**ed.
6. I don't usually wear styli**sh sh**oes. They're not as comfortable as my sneakers.

C *Class activity* Ask your classmates questions. Find someone who agrees with each statement.

"Do you like big glasses?" ***"Yes, I do. I think they're just as stylish as small glasses."***

Lesson **B** **Fashion**

1 Building language

A Listen. Why doesn't Ben like the jacket? Practice the conversation.

Yoko Oh, don't you just love this jacket? I mean, isn't it great?
Ben Hmm. I don't know.
Yoko Don't you like it? I think it's really nice.
Ben It's OK. It's kind of bright.
Yoko But don't you like the style? It'd look good on you, don't you think?
Ben Well, maybe.
Yoko Well, don't you want to try it on at least?
Ben Not really. And anyway, isn't it a little expensive?
Yoko Oh, isn't it on sale?
Ben No. It's full price. The sale rack is over there. Hey, look at those jackets. Aren't they great?

B How does Yoko actually say these things? Underline what she says in the conversation.

1. I love this jacket!
2. I'm surprised you don't like it.
3. I think you should try it on.

2 Grammar *Negative questions*

When you want or expect someone to agree with you, you can use negative questions to:

Express an opinion	***Suggest an idea***	***Show surprise***
Isn't this jacket great?	**Isn't** it a little expensive?	**Isn't** it on sale?
Don't you think it's great?	**Don't** you think it's too bright?	**Don't** you like it?
Don't you just love it?	It'd look good, **don't** you think?	

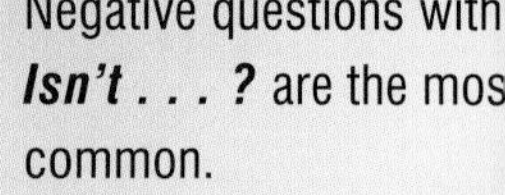

Negative questions with ***Isn't . . . ?*** are the most common.

Look at the rest of Yoko and Ben's conversation. Rewrite the underlined sentences as negative questions. Then practice with a partner.

Ben Look at this one. I think it's neat.
Yoko Well, I'm not sure about the style. I think it's a bit boring.
Ben No, I like it. And it fits perfectly, I think.
Yoko Um . . . maybe it's a bit tight.
Ben No, it's just right. I'm surprised you don't like it. And anyway, it's not as expensive. I think I'll get it!
Yoko Well, I think you should look around a bit more.

Isn't it neat? / Don't you think it's neat?

3 Building vocabulary

A ***Pair work*** Read the product descriptions on this Web page, and take turns describing the items in the photos.

Search
GO
Outerwear
Shirts
Pants
Footwear
Accessories
Activewear
Kids
For Him
For Her
Gift Cards
FREE SHIPPING over $50
1. Choose from our huge selection of men's and women's **leather** and **suede** jackets.
2. Luxury **cashmere** scarves and **silk** ties make perfect gifts.
3. Men's **wool turtleneck** and **V-neck** sweaters.
4. Women's **long-sleeved cotton** tops, available in a range of **solid colors.** Shown here in **neon** green, **dark** green, and **light** green.
5. Looking for **denim** jeans? Whether you want **boot-cut** or **flared, fitted** or **baggy** – we have jeans to fit you!
6. Women's **short-sleeved striped** shirts in **polyester. Floral-print** and **plaid** shirts also available.
7. **Rubber** boots in a variety of patterns. Shown here in **turquoise** with a **polka-dot** pattern.

Word sort → **B** Complete the chart with words from the Web page, and add ideas. Then compare with a partner. Can you use any of these words to describe what you and your classmates are wearing?

Colors	*Patterns*	*Materials*		*Styles*	
neon green	striped	leather		V-neck	

About you → **C** ***Group work*** Talk about the items on the Web page above. Discuss the following questions. Try to use negative questions where possible.

- Which items do you really like? Are they in style right now?
- Do you like the colors? How about the materials?
- Would they look good on you or someone in the group?
- How much would you pay for them? What would be a reasonable price?

"Isn't that leather jacket great?" *"I guess so, but don't you think it's a bit out of style?"*

4 Vocabulary notebook *Blue suede shoes*

See page 20 for a useful way to log and learn vocabulary.

Lesson C He has really broad tastes.

1 Conversation strategy *Summarizing things people say*

A Which response summarizes what A says?

A *A lot of bands sound the same to me. I can't tell one band from another.*
B *I know. ________________ .*
a. They can't play their instruments. b. They sound terrible. c. They're all alike.

Now listen. What do you find out about Omar's brother?

Tracy *So, what are we looking for? I mean, what kind of music does your brother like?*
Omar *He likes rock, hip-hop, jazz, . . .*
Tracy *Gosh. He has really broad tastes in music.*
Omar *Yeah. I'm not sure what to get him. He has hundreds of CDs already.*
Tracy *He has a big collection, then.*
Omar *Oh, yeah. And he knows a lot about music, too – like song lyrics, what albums are in the charts, when bands had their first hits, . . .*
Tracy *Sounds like he's a walking encyclopedia.*
Omar *Yeah. He knows everything about this stuff!*
Tracy *Now, does he read music magazines? Because you could get him a year's subscription to one.*
Omar *Oh, yeah. That's a great idea. I think I'll do that.*

Notice how Tracy summarizes the things Omar says. It shows she's involved in the conversation and is following what Omar is saying. Find more examples.

"Gosh. He has really broad tastes in music."

B Match each statement with the best response. Then practice with a partner.

1. I like music with a good rhythm, something catchy. ____
2. I hate listening to music on the radio – they always play the same stuff. ____
3. I like songs that mean something, with words you can remember. ____
4. Rap is really clever, the way it rhymes and tells a story. ____
5. I have every record that The Beatles ever made. ____

a. I know. It's like poetry.
b. Yeah. Good lyrics are important
c. Wow. That's a big collection.
d. Right. There's not much variety.
e. Uh-huh. You like a good beat.

SELF-STUDY AUDIO CD CD-ROM

2 Strategy plus *Now*

Now is often used to introduce a follow-up question. It shows that you want to move the conversation on to a different aspect of a topic.

Now, does he read music magazines?

In conversation . . .

Now is one of the top 100 words. About 20% of the uses of ***now*** are to introduce questions.

A Complete the conversations with the questions in the box. Then practice with a partner.

do you have satellite radio	do you play any musical instruments	do you listen to music when you're reading or working

1. *A* Do you like classical music?
   B Yeah. I like most types of music. Classical, jazz, folk – anything, really.
   A So you have pretty broad tastes. Now, ______________ ?
   B Not really. I took piano for a while when I was a kid.

2. *A* Do you go to concerts at all?
   B Occasionally. I mean, it's nice to hear live music, but it can get expensive.
   A Yeah, I know. Now, ______________ ? They often have live bands.
   B No, I don't have it yet. I don't subscribe to it.

3. *A* Do you have music on all the time at home?
   B Pretty much. It's the first thing I do when I come home – turn on some music.
   A Oh, me too. Now, ______________ ?
   B No, I can't have it on when I need to concentrate on something.

About you → **B** Ask and answer the questions. Use your own information.

3 Listening *My music collection*

A Listen to Jason talk to his co-worker about music. Circle the correct information.

1. He owns about **600 / 110** CDs.
2. He plays his CDs in a **normal / special** CD player.
3. He keeps the liner notes about his CDs in **a catalog / the CD cases**.
4. He has copied **some / all** of his CDs onto an MP3 player.
5. He thinks he'll probably **keep / get rid of** his CDs.

B Listen again to excerpts from the conversation. Choose the best response to each one.

1. a. So you have broad tastes. b. So you're pretty choosy.
2. a. So you have a small collection. b. So you have a fairly big collection.
3. a. That's enough. b. That's not nearly enough.
4. a. So it's difficult to use? b. So it's easy to use, like a jukebox?

Personal style

1 Reading

A Look at the photos of the woman below. What do you think her tastes are in clothes? jewelry? home decor? Make word webs.

miniskirts — **clothes** **jewelry** **home decor**

B Read the interview. Were your guesses correct? Do you have anything in common with Lesley? What?

A free spirit!

An interview with Lesley Koustaff in New York about her very individual tastes

How would you describe your style in clothes? Don't you have some pretty unusual clothes?
Yes, I do have some unusual clothes . . . and jewelry! I suppose my style would be called eclectic. I like to collect clothing and jewelry from various countries and combine them. So I suppose the result is an interesting and different look.

Don't you think clothes say a lot about the kind of person you are?
Absolutely. I think we express who we are through our clothes – our personalities are reflected in our clothes.

What do your clothes say about you?
That I am outgoing and an individual – not one of the group. I suppose also that I am creative and a free spirit.

What's your favorite outfit?
My black miniskirt and jacket. I wear it with clunky shoes, lipstick-patterned tights, and very big earrings and a big pin. Jewelry is as important to me as my clothes. I have a handmade shawl made by local people in South Africa that I wear over the jacket.

What kinds of styles and colors don't you wear?
Anything that is very feminine. I don't wear lacy clothes. I love color, so I don't think about whether or not a color looks good on me. I wear every color under the sun . . . sometimes all at once!

What would you never wear?
A backless evening gown and stiletto heels.

What's your taste in music? Don't you have a lot of African music?
Yes, I have a lot of African music – I love the beat and spirit of the music. It comes from the heart. I like to listen to music from a lot of different countries. And I love jazz, classical, and Latin music.

Why don't you tell me about the style of your home? It's so calm in here.
Well, I do *feng shui* – you know, the Chinese art of placing things in harmony – so I took great care in where I placed my furniture. The things I have in my home reflect Africa and Asia, where I spent most of my life, . . . so they are really a part of me, not just items. Each piece has a story. I have a water fountain running 24 hours a day – I love the sound of water and find it very calming.

C Find the underlined words in the interview. What do you think Lesley means when she uses those words? What helped you guess the meaning?

1. Her (clothing) style is <u>eclectic</u>.	a. strange	b. varied	c. exciting
2. Clothes <u>reflect</u> our personalities.	a. show	b. hide	c. develop
3. She is a <u>free spirit</u>.	a. happy	b. sad	c. independent
4. She doesn't like <u>feminine</u> styles.	a. girlish	b. unusual	c. plain
5. She wears every color <u>under the sun</u>.	a. like yellow	b. outdoors	c. that exists

2 Listening and speaking *What's your thing?*

A Listen to four people talk about their tastes. Which two topics does each person talk about?

books **cars** **clothes** **food** **friends** **furniture** **hairstyles** **music**

1. Charlie ________ ________
2. Louisa ________ ________
3. Frankie ________ ________
4. Hugo ________ ________

B Listen again and answer the questions. Who do you have the most in common with? Compare ideas with a partner.

1. Who enjoys reading about his or her interest?
2. Who has simple tastes in food?
3. Who's not very interested in fashion?
4. Who likes to pay more and buy top-quality items?

"I guess I'm a bit like Charlie. You know, I don't like to . . ."

3 Writing and speaking *Style interview*

A Choose a classmate to interview about his or her personal style. Choose five questions from the article on page 18, or make up five of your own. Write them down.

B Exchange questions with your partner. Write answers to your partner's questions.

How would you describe your tastes in clothes? Don't you wear a lot of designer labels?

Absolutely! I've always been interested in fashion – clothes, accessories, and hairstyles.

Help note

Punctuation

- Use commas (**,**) in lists.
  *My clothes are colorful**,** fun**,** and artsy.*
- Use a dash (**–**) to add or explain more about something.
  *I have a lot of African music **–** I love the beat and spirit . . .*
- Use an exclamation mark (**!**) for emphasis.
  *I wear every color under the sun . . . sometimes all at once**!***

C ***Pair work*** Now read your partner's answers. Ask questions to find out more information.

4 Free talk *What's popular?*

See ***Free talk 2*** at the back of the book for more speaking practice.

Blue suede shoes

Learning tip *Labeling pictures*

When you want to learn a new set of vocabulary, find and label pictures illustrating the new words. For example, you can use a fashion magazine to label items of clothing, styles, colors, patterns, and materials.

Shades of blue

The top ways of describing ***blue*** in conversation are:

1. ***navy*** blue
2. ***dark*** blue
3. ***royal*** blue
4. ***bright***
5. ***light*** b
6. ***deep*** b

1 What styles of clothing, colors, and patterns can you see in the picture? What materials do you think the clothes are made of? Label the picture with words from the box and other words you know.

✓baggy	flared	long-sleeved	silk	turtleneck
cotton	floral-print	neon orange	striped	V-neck
dark brown	leather	polka-dot	✓suede	wool
fitted	light blue	short-sleeved	turquoise	

2 *Word builder* Find out what these words mean. Then find an example of each one in the picture above, and add labels.

ankle-length	gold	navy blue
beige	maroon	plastic
crew-neck	mauve	tweed

On your own

Find a fashion magazine, and label as many of the different styles, materials, patterns, and colors as you can in ten minutes.

Unit 3

/orld cultures

ıit 3, you learn how to . . .

e simple present passive to talk about traditional things.
ɔout manners using verb + *-ing* and *to* + verb.
ɔout different cultures and customs.
‹pressions like *in fact* to sound more direct when you speak.
f course to give information that is not surprising,
show you understand or agree.

1

2

3

4

5

6

Before you begin . . .

What are some of the cultural traditions in your country? Think of a typical . . .

- dish or drink.
- song or type of music.
- festival.
- costume.
- symbol.
- handicraft.

Traditional things

WHAT NOT TO MISS . . .

We asked people: What's one thing you shouldn't miss on a visit to . . . ?

SOUTH KOREA

"Oh, Korean food! We have so many different dishes. One typical dish is *kim-bap*. It's made with rice and vegetables, and wrapped in dried seaweed. And it's eaten cold. It's delicious."

– *Min Hee Park*

PERU

"Well, Peru has some beautiful handicrafts. A lot of the are exported nowadays, and they're sold all over the world. But it's still worth visiting a local market. These earrings are made locally. They're made of silver."

– *Elena Camac*

JAPAN

"A Japanese festival like the Sapporo Ice Festival – that's really worth seeing. It's held every February. They have all these sculptures that are carved out of ice – and they're carved by teams from all over the world. It's amazing."

– *Sachio Ito*

AUSTRALIA

"Oh, you should go to a performance of traditional Aboriginal music. They play this instrument – it's calle a *didgeridoo*. It's made out of a hollow piece of wood an painted by hand. It makes a really interesting sound."

– *Robert Fl*

1 Getting started

A Listen to four people talk about their country's culture. What four aspects of culture do they talk about?

Figure it out

B Rewrite the sentences below, but keep the same meaning. Use the comments above to help you.

1. You eat *kim-bap* cold. — *Kim-bap* ________________ cold.
2. People make earrings like these locally. — Earrings like these ________________ locally.
3. They paint *didgeridoos* by hand. — *Didgeridoos* ________________ by hand.

2 Grammar *The simple present passive*

Use the passive when the "doer" of the action is not known or not important.

Active	**Passive**
How do they make *kim-bap*?	How **is** *kim-bap* **made**?
They make it with rice and vegetables.	It**'s made** with rice and vegetables.
Do they eat it hot or cold?	**Is** it **eaten** hot or cold?
They eat it cold. They don't eat it hot.	It**'s eaten** cold. It**'s** not **eaten** hot.
They carve the sculptures out of ice.	The sculptures **are carved** out of ice.

If the "doer" of the action is important, you can introduce it with by.

The sculptures **are carved by** teams from all over the world.

In conversation . . .

The most common passive verbs are ***made***, ***done***, and ***called***.

About you

Complete the questions about your country's culture with the simple present passive. Then ask and answer the questions with a partner.

1. What's the national anthem? When is it sung (sing)?
2. What's your favorite traditional dish? How ____________ (make)? What ____________ (serve) with?
3. What do you think are the most important festivals? When ____________ (celebrate)?
4. Is there a national costume? When ____________ (wear)?
5. What are your national sports? ____________ (play) by both men and women?
6. Is there any traditional folk music? Where ____________ (play)?

"The national anthem is called 'O Canada,' and it's sung at special events."

3 Speaking naturally *Silent syllables*

ev(e)ry *diff(e)rent* *int(e)resting* *veg(e)table*

A Listen and repeat the words above. Notice how the unstressed vowels are not pronounced.

B Listen to people talk about their cities. Cross out the vowel that is not pronounced in the underlined words. Then read the sentences aloud to a partner.

1. We're known for our chocolate, which is sold all over the world. If you're really interested, you can visit a factory to learn about the history of chocolate and how it's made.
2. The average temperature here in summer is almost 40°C, so it's much cooler to live underground. It's definitely something different for travelers!
3. If you want a camera, then you have to shop here. Practically every brand of electronic and computer goods is displayed here!
4. Emeralds are mined all over the world, but our region has some of the best and most valuable stones. They're mostly exported and made into jewelry.

C Listen again. Can you guess which place each person is talking about? Write the number. What is your region or city known for? Tell the class.

Akihabara, Japan ___ Boyacá, Colombia ___ Broc, Switzerland ___ Coober Pedy, Australia ___

Manners

1 Building vocabulary and grammar

A Listen. Are these statements about manners true in your country? Check (✓) true or false.

	True	False
1. **Eating food** on a subway or bus is bad manners.	☐	☐
2. It's rude to **cut in line**.	☐	☐
3. You should try to **keep your voice down** in public.	☐	☐
4. You can offend someone by not **bowing** or **shaking hands** when you meet.	☐	☐
5. People might **stare** at you for **walking around barefoot**.	☐	☐
6. **Having an argument** in public is considered bad manners.	☐	☐
7. It's impolite to walk into someone's home without **taking off your shoes**.	☐	☐
8. **Showing affection** in public – **holding hands** or **kissing** – is inappropriate.	☐	☐
9. You should try not to **stand too close** to people. It's considered rude.	☐	☐
10. It's acceptable not to **tip** cab drivers.	☐	☐
11. You should be careful not to **point at people**.	☐	☐
12. It's customary to **bargain** with street vendors to get something cheaper, but it's not acceptable to do this in a store.	☐	☐

Word sort

B What behaviors are considered acceptable in your country? Complete the lists with ideas from above. Add other ideas. Then compare with a partner.

Do . . .	Don't . . .
take your shoes off in the house.	stand too close to people.

Figure it out

C Can you complete these sentences? Use *to* + verb or verb + *-ing*. Compare with a partner.

1. ________________ in line is bad manners.
2. You can offend people by ________________ affection in public.
3. It's rude not ________________ or shake hands when you meet someone.

2 Grammar *Verb + -ing and to + verb; position of not*

Verb + -ing as a subject
Eating in public is bad manners.
Not shaking hands is impolite.

Verb + -ing after prepositions
You can offend people by **eating** in public.
People might stare at you for **not shaking** hands.

to + verb after It's . . .
It's bad manners **to eat** in public.
It's impolite **not to shake** hands.

Position of not

Not comes before the word it negates.
Be careful **not** to point at people.
You can offend people by **not** bowing.

Notice the difference in meaning:
It's acceptable **not** to tip cab drivers. =
It's optional.
It's **not** acceptable to tip cab drivers. =
You shouldn't do it.

A Complete these sentences about visiting someone's home with either verb + *-ing* or *to* + verb.

1. It's impolite to go to a friend's home for dinner without ________________ (bring) a gift.
2. ________________ (arrive) a little late is acceptable.
3. It's not a good idea ________________ (invite) a friend without asking the host.
4. It's polite ________________ (compliment) the host's cooking.
5. If you don't like something your host serves, it's best ________________ (not say) anything and leave it.
6. It's customary ________________ (not ask) for second helpings of food.
7. ________________ (talk) with your mouth full is considered rude.
8. It's acceptable ________________ (not finish) the food on your plate.
9. ________________ (take) a call on your cell phone during dinner is bad manners.
10. You can upset your host by ________________ (not leave) until it's very late.

B ***Group work*** Discuss the statements above. Which do you agree with?

A ***I think it's OK not to bring a gift if it's a friend. What do you think?***
B ***Well, actually, I think it's a good idea to bring something, even if it's something small.***
C ***Yeah, I agree. Bringing a gift is good manners.***

C ***Group work*** Can you think of other advice for showing good manners in someone's home? Make a list to share with the class.

3 Vocabulary notebook *Travel etiquette*

See page 30 for a new way to log and learn vocabulary.

Lesson C To be honest, . . .

1 Conversation strategy *Sounding more direct*

A **Which of these answers sound more direct? Which sound less direct?**

What would you miss about home if you moved abroad?

a. I'd definitely miss my family.
b. I guess I'd miss the people.
c. To be honest, I don't think I'd miss too much.
d. I'd probably miss the culture.

Now listen to Hilda and David. What would David miss if he left Brazil?

Hilda ***So, when you're living here, do you miss hom***
David ***Um, I don't miss too much, to be honest. Um, miss my family, of course. . . .***
Hilda ***Right.***
David ***But I definitely don't miss the food! Um, I mis my family. That's about it.***
Hilda ***So, if you went back home, would you miss lo of things about Brazil?***
David ***Oh, yeah. I'd absolutely miss the food here. Yeah. But actually, I think the biggest thing would be . . . it would be weird for me to live a country where I knew the language already where all I have to do is work. I just don't see a challenge in that. You know, here every day is a challenge, speaking the language.***
Hilda ***Uh-huh.***
David ***In fact, living back home would be boring, I think. I honestly don't know what I'd do.***

Notice **that when David wants to sound more direct or assertive, he uses expressions like these. Find examples in the conversation.**

absolutely, definitely, really, actually, certainly, honestly, in fact, to be honest, to tell you the truth

About you

B Use the expressions given to make these statements more direct. Compare with a partner. Then discuss each statement. Do you agree?

1. If I lived abroad, I'd miss my friends. (definitely)
2. I wouldn't miss the food. (to be honest)
3. I'd enjoy learning a new language. (actually)
4. Shopping would be a challenge. (certainly)
5. I wouldn't be homesick. (to tell you the truth)
6. I wouldn't enjoy living in a different culture. (honestly)

A ***If I lived abroad, I'd definitely miss my friends!***
B ***Oh, me too. I'd miss everyone, to be honest.***

2 Strategy plus *of course*

Of course **usually means "This idea is not surprising. It's what you expect."**

I miss my family, of course.

You can also use *Of course* in responses to show you agree or understand.

A I really miss my family.
B Of course.

Note: Be careful when you use *of course*. It can sound abrupt or rude as an answer to a question.

A Do you miss your family?
B Oh, yes, I really do.
(NOT ~~Of course~~.)

In conversation . . .

Of course is one of the top 50 expressions.

A Listen to the questions and answers. Does the expression *of course* in the answer sound polite or impolite? Check (✓) the boxes.

	Polite	Impolite
1. *A* Do you think living in another country would be exciting? *B* Absolutely. Of course, I'd probably feel homesick at times.	✓	☐
2. *A* What would you miss most if you moved to another country? *B* Well, I'd miss the food and, of course, all my friends.	✓	☐
3. *A* Would you miss your parents if you were living away from home? *B* Of course. Wouldn't you?	☐	✓
4. *A* What would you take with you to remind you of home? *B* Oh, I'd definitely take my guitar and, of course, all my favorite CDs.	✓	☐
5. *A* Would you try to learn the language before moving to a new country? *B* Of course. You really have to learn the language.	☐	✓
6. *A* How would you keep in touch with everyone? *B* I'd e-mail regularly, of course, and I'd call them as often as I could.	✓	☐

About you → **B *Pair work*** Ask and answer the questions, giving your own answers. Use *of course* in your answers, but be careful how you use it.

3 Listening and speaking *Away from home*

A Listen to Frances talk about being away from home. How would she answer these questions?

1. Why are you living away from home?
2. Do your parents miss you? Why (not)?
3. How do you keep in touch? How often?
4. What do you miss about home?

About you → **B *Group work*** Think about a time you were away from home. Who and what did you miss? How did you keep in touch? Tell the group about your experience.

"When I went away to college, I really missed my family."

Lesson D Proverbs

1 Reading

A A popular proverb in English is "Don't count your chickens before they hatch." Can you guess what it means?

B Read the article. Are any of these proverbs familiar to you?

Counting Chickens

The world's timeless proverbs offer great wisdom – which we sometimes turn into folly.

By Fred D. Baldwin

Whenever I find myself banking on future good fortune, I'm apt to think, "Don't count your chickens before they hatch."

Germans express the same idea like this: "You have to catch the hare before you can roast him." The French say: "You can't sell the bear's skin until you've caught him." A Japanese version is almost identical, except that the animal to be caught is a *tanuki*, which resembles a raccoon.

Proverbs – bite-sized chunks of popular wisdom – abound in all languages. We use proverbs to make points more convincingly and more memorably than most of us could otherwise manage. We also use proverbs because they lend a measure of authority to our opinions, suggesting that what we are saying is simply common sense.

Yet proverbial wisdom can be contradictory. We warn the cautious against hesitation with "He who hesitates is lost," but we also warn the bold, "Look before you leap." We may say that "Absence makes the heart grow fonder," but we also say, "Out of sight, out of mind." When we want help, we say, "Many hands make light work." When we don't want it, we grumble that "Too many cooks spoil the broth."

"Proverbs are not universal truths," says Wolfgang Mieder, professor of German and folklore at the University of Vermont. "Proverbs represent life; therefore, there will be contradictory proverbs."

That proverbs serve as small, prefabricated parts to conversation makes them useful to travelers. If your fluency in a language is limited, a memorized proverb can come in handy when encountering situations likely to occur on any trip – a late arrival, an unexpected turn of events, or perhaps the need to acknowledge a blunder.

I admit, however, to having once spent several uncomfortable minutes in Japan after having come out with "The child of a frog is a frog," the Japanese version of "The apple doesn't fall far from the tree" – only to be met with blank, uncomprehending stares. It seems that the Japanese word for "frog" sounds much like the Japanese verb "to return." My hosts must have thought that I was babbling about a B movie – something like *The Return of Frog-Boy.*

As we often say, anybody can make a mistake. Or, as a Japanese proverb has it, "Even monkeys fall from trees." When people at the table finally grasped what I was trying to say, my recitation did indeed relax them – doubled them up with laughter, in fact. It gave me a perfect opening for "Fall down seven times, get up eight." That's the Japanese version of "If at first you don't succeed, . . . try, try again."

Fred D. Baldwin enjoyed writing this article, citing the Japanese proverb "To teach is to learn." Baldwin resides in Carlisle, Pennsylvania, U.S.A.

Source: *Attaché* magazine

C Find English proverbs in the article with these meanings. Do you have similar proverbs in your language? Discuss with a partner.

1. Never assume you're going to be lucky.
2. When you miss someone, you love him or her more.
3. Lots of people make a job easier.
4. Never give up.

D Read the article again. Can you find these things? Compare answers with a partner.

1. two reasons why people use proverbs
2. three pairs of proverbs with opposite meanings
3. three situations in which travelers might use proverbs
4. the reason why the author's attempt at using a proverb didn't work
5. a proverb in English and in another language with the same meaning

2 Listening and writing *Favorite proverbs*

A Can you guess the meaning of the proverbs below? Discuss with a partner.

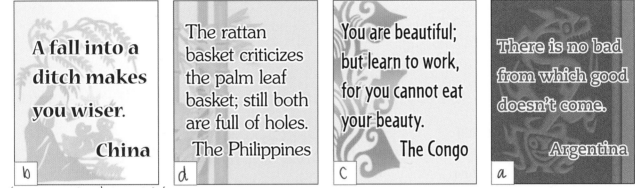

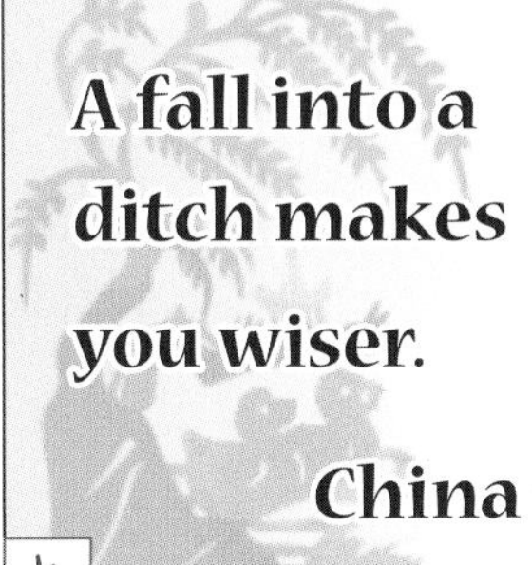

A fall into a ditch makes you wiser.
China

The rattan basket criticizes the palm leaf basket; still both are full of holes.
The Philippines

You are beautiful; but learn to work, for you cannot eat your beauty.
The Congo

There is no bad from which good doesn't come.
Argentina

B Listen to four people talk about their favorite proverbs. Number the proverbs above.

C Match each proverb above with a similar English proverb below. Write the number. Then listen again as someone responds to each proverb, and check your answers.

a. Every cloud has a silver lining. ___
b. Once bitten, twice shy. ___
c. Beauty is only skin deep. ___
d. It's like the pot calling the kettle black. ___

D What is your favorite proverb? Choose one and write a short article about it. What does it mean? Why do you like it? How does it relate to your life?

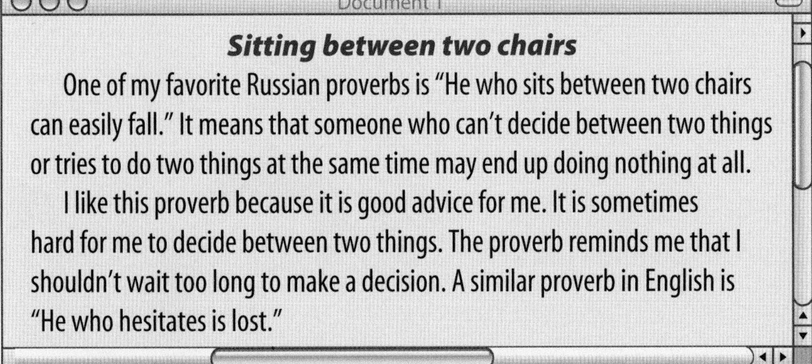
Document 1

Sitting between two chairs

One of my favorite Russian proverbs is "He who sits between two chairs can easily fall." It means that someone who can't decide between two things or tries to do two things at the same time may end up doing nothing at all.

I like this proverb because it is good advice for me. It is sometimes hard for me to decide between two things. The proverb reminds me that I shouldn't wait too long to make a decision. A similar proverb in English is "He who hesitates is lost."

Help note

Useful expressions

One of my favorite proverbs is . . .
It's often said when . . .
It means that . . .
I like it because . . .
A similar proverb in English is ". . ."
The proverb ". . ." expresses the same idea.

E Read your classmates' articles. Which proverb do you think is the most interesting?

3 Free talk *Local customs*

See ***Free talk 3*** for more speaking practice.

Vocabulary notebook

Travel etiquette

Learning tip *Finding more examples*

When you learn new expressions, try to find more examples in magazines, in newspapers, and on the Internet. To find examples on different Web sites, type the expressions into an Internet search engine, putting quotation marks (" ") around it.

Search

Web Images Groups News Local

"don't point your foot"

Web

Dos and Don'ts in Thailand
... when sitting opposite someone, **don't point your foot** at . . .
www.thailand.com - 12k - Cached - Similar pages

drills - racquetball
Don't point your foot in the direction . . .
www.racquetballdrills.com - 12k - Cached - Similar pages

1 Look at the cultural facts about different countries. Complete the sentences using the words and expressions in the box.

to show	to keep your voice down	to take off	bowing	kissing	having an argument
to cut in line	to shake hands	to hold hands	standing	eating	walking around barefoot

1. In Japan, ____________ is customary when two people introduce themselves.
2. In the U.S.A., it's polite ____________ firmly when you are introduced to a business colleague.
3. In Korea, ____________ food on the subway is considered rude.
4. In many places of worship in Asia, it's polite ____________ your hat and shoes.
5. In India, it's customary ____________ with your friends as you walk together.
6. In Spain, ____________ very close to someone when you are talking is acceptable.
7. In Chile, people often say hello by ____________ each other on the cheek.
8. In Australia, ____________ is acceptable at beach resorts, but not in public buildings.
9. In Saudi Arabia, it's offensive ____________ the bottom of your foot to someone.
10. In Taiwan, ____________ in public is considered impolite. It's better ____________.
11. In Great Britain, it's considered rude ____________. You should always wait your turn.

2 ***Word builder*** Find out the meaning of these words and expressions. Then write a real etiquette tip about each for your culture.

blow your nose **burp** **offer your seat to someone** **swear**

On your own

Choose a country you would like to visit. Find a travel guide on that country, or go on the Internet. Make a list of 6 things you should or shouldn't do when you travel there.

Touchstone checkpoint Units 1–3

1 Is it polite?

A Complete the questions with the correct forms of the verbs.

1. Would you ever consider ____________ (not tip) a server in a restaurant?
2. Do you remember ____________ (stare) at people when you were little?
3. Do you feel it's rude ____________ (not say) hello to your neighbors?
4. Is ____________ (hold hands) OK on a first date?
5. Do you bother ____________ (bargain) with street vendors when the items are already very cheap?
6. Do you ever offer ____________ (help) people on the bus or subway with their bags?
7. Have you and a friend ever ended up ____________ (argue) in public?
8. Have you ever offended someone without ____________ (intend) ____________ (be) rude?

B ***Pair work*** Ask and answer the questions. Show that you understand your partner's answers by summarizing what he or she says.

"I'd never consider not tipping – I used to be a server myself." ***"So you always tip the server."***

2 Think, Bob, think!

A Complete the conversation with the correct forms of the verbs.

Officer ______ you ______ (see) these people before?
Bob Yes, they're my neighbors. They ______ (live) upstairs.
Officer How long ______ they ____________ (live) there?
Bob I guess I ______ (know) them for six months. They ______ (move) here in August.
Officer When ______ you last ______ (see) them?
Bob Um, about a week ago, I think. Last Tuesday.
Officer What ______ they ______ (do) when you ______ (see) them?
Bob Well, as I ____________ (come) home, they ____________ (carry) a big suitcase to the car.
Officer ______ you ______ (speak) to them?
Bob I ______ (say), "Hi! Where ______ you ______ (go)?" And they ______ (reply), "On vacation."
Officer What time ______ they finally ______ (leave)?
Bob Oh, um, it was pretty late, around 11 at night, I guess.
Officer Can you remember what they ____________ (wear)?
Bob Let me think. . . .

B Write Bob's answer to the police officer's last question. How much detail can you give? Compare with a partner.

3 Can you complete this conversation?

A Complete the conversation with the words and expressions in the box. Practice the conversation.

✓definitely	don't you think	now	of course	these	this	to be honest

Anna Bella used to live in Japan. You loved living there, right?
Bella Oh, definitely. I lived there for nine years, working for a Japanese advertising company.
Chris Nine years? Wow! Didn't you ever get homesick?
Bella Occasionally. But, ________, I didn't really miss living at home. I was too busy. I mean, ________ I missed my family.
Chris Oh, I bet you did. ________, how did you get that job? Did they hire you over here, or . . . ?
Bella Actually, I was already in Japan on an exchange program, staying with ________ family. And the father starts bringing home all ________ documents from his work to translate into English. Anyway, I started helping him, and his company ended up hiring me.
Anna And they transferred her here. It's a cool story, ________?

B ***Pair work*** Choose a topic and have a conversation. Ask and answer questions.

- something difficult you did once
- an interesting experience you had
- a time you missed someone
- an unusual person you once met

4 As bad as that?

Pair work Compare these things using *(not) as . . . as.* Try to use negative questions to give opinions or to suggest ideas.

- folk music / rock music
- baked potatoes / fries
- old buildings / new buildings
- cheap watches / expensive watches

A ***Folk music isn't as popular as rock music. You don't hear it as much.***
B ***But don't you think it's just as good? I like folk as much as rock.***

5 Guess the dish!

A Write questions in the simple present passive, using these words. Then think of a traditional dish, and answer the questions.

1. eat / hot or cold
2. When / eat
3. How / cook
4. What / make / with
5. What / serve / with
6. What / call

B ***Pair work*** Take turns asking and answering the questions. Can you guess your partner's dish before question 6?

Self-check

How sure are you about these areas? Circle the percentages.

grammar
20% 40% 60% 80% 100%
vocabulary
20% 40% 60% 80% 100%
conversation strategies
20% 40% 60% 80% 100%

Study plan

What do you want to review? Circle the lessons.

grammar
1A 1B 2A 2B 3A 3B
vocabulary
1A 1B 2A 2B 3A 3B
conversation strategies
1C 2C 3C

Unit 4

Socializing

In Unit 4, you learn how to . . .

- talk about things you *are supposed to* do.
- use *was / were supposed to* and *was / were going to* to talk about things you didn't do.
- talk about going out and socializing.
- use different expressions with the verb *get*.
- use questions in the form of statements to check your understanding.
- use *so* in different ways, such as to start or close a topic.

2

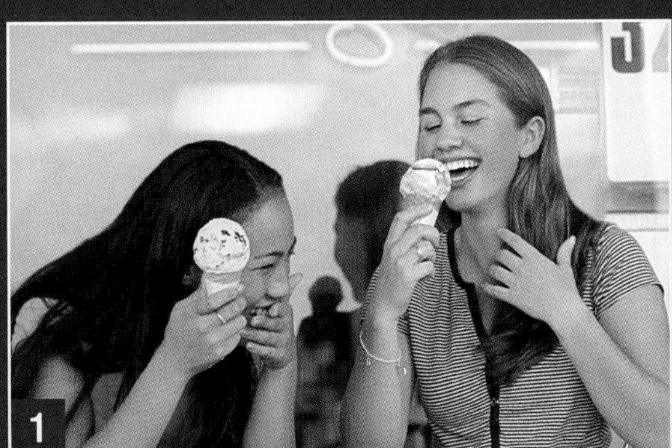
1

4

3

Before you begin . . .

Where are some good places to go out with friends?

Is it expensive to go out in your city?

Who do you usually socialize with?

Party time

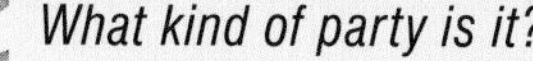

Marco: Are you going to Brad and Gayle's party?

Anna: Well, I wasn't going to go, but maybe I will. I'm supposed to be studying for an exam. Are you going?

Marco: Yeah. The party's at their house, right? Do you know where they live?

Anna: Not exactly. Brad was going to call and give me directions, but he didn't. Maybe Ellen knows.

Ellen: What kind of party is it?

Phil: I think it's supposed to be a barbecue.

Ellen: That'll be fun. Have you heard the weather forecast?

Phil: Yeah. I heard it's supposed to be a really nice evening.

Anwar: Are we supposed to bring anything?

Sue: I don't think so. I was going to make some potato salad, but I didn't have time.

Anwar: Well, I bought them a box of chocolates. Do you think that'll be OK?

Sue: I don't know. Isn't Brad on a diet? He's not supposed to eat stuff like that. But Gayle will like them.

Patty: Jen and Martin are late. They were supposed to pick me up at 7:00.

Junko: Gosh, it's 7:30 already. Maybe they forgot. Do you want me to come and get you? I can take you home, too.

Patty: That'd be great. But I'm supposed to be at work early tomorrow, so I can't stay late.

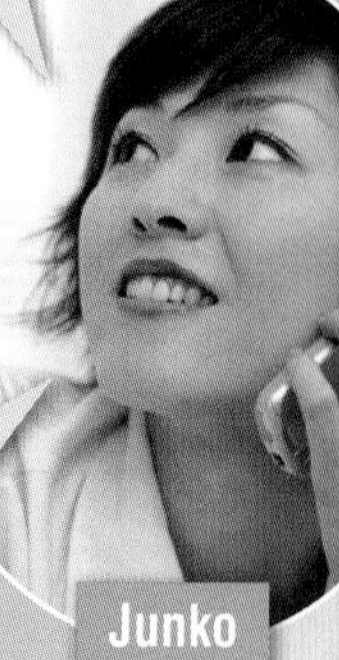

Junko: That's OK. I think the party's supposed to end at 11:00, but we can leave a bit earlier.

1 Getting started

A Listen. Brad and Gayle are having a party tonight, and their friends are getting ready. What do you find out about the party?

Figure it out → **B** How might Brad and Gayle's friends say the things below? Replace the underlined words with an expression each person has already used above.

1. *Phil* They say it's going to be really warm.
2. *Sue* Brad shouldn't eat chocolate.
3. *Patty* I have to get up early tomorrow.
4. *Anna* I should be working on a paper.
5. *Patty* Jen and Martin agreed to be here by 7:00.
6. *Sue* I intended to make a dessert, but I didn't.

2 Grammar *be supposed to; was / were going to*

***Be supposed to* can mean "They say . . . ."**	It's **supposed to** be a barbecue. It's **supposed to** rain later.
It can also mean "have to" or "should."	I'm **supposed to** work tomorrow. He's **not supposed to** eat chocolate.
It can contrast what should happen with what does or will happen.	I'm **supposed to** be studying for an exam (but I'm not). I'm **not supposed to** stay out late (but maybe I will).
***Was / Were supposed to* can mean what was expected didn't or won't happen.**	They **were supposed to** come at 7:00 (but they didn't). I **wasn't supposed to** go by myself (but I'll have to).
***Was / Were going to* has a similar meaning and can also mean "intended to."**	He **was going to** give us directions (but he didn't). I **wasn't going to** go to the party (but I guess I will).

In conversation . . .

Over 60% of uses of ***supposed to*** are in the present tense. About 10% are negative.

A Complete the conversations with the correct form of *be supposed to* or *was / were going to* and the verb. Sometimes more than one answer is possible. Practice with a partner.

1. *A* Are there any restaurants around here that ________ (be) really good?
   B Yeah, the new Turkish one around the corner ________ (be) excellent. And there's a good Italian restaurant two blocks away. We ________ (go) there last Friday, but I had to work late.
2. *A* The weather ________ (be) beautiful this weekend. Do you have any plans?
   B Yeah, I ________ (go) to my parents' house. They're planning a surprise party for my birthday, and I ________ (not / know) about it, but my sister told me about it last week.
3. *A* How was your weekend? Did you do anything fun?
   B Not really. My friend ________ (come) and have dinner at my place, and then we ________ (see) a movie, but she got sick and couldn't make it. How about you?
   A Well, I ________ (not / do) anything because I had to study, but I went out anyway.

About you → **B *Pair work*** Ask and answer the questions. Give your own answers.

3 Talk about it *Weekend fun*

Group work Discuss the questions about this weekend.

- What's the weather supposed to be like?
- Are there any upcoming events that are supposed to be fun?
- Are there any new movies that are supposed to be good?
- Are you supposed to go anywhere or see anyone in particular?
- Is there anything you were going to do last weekend that you're going to do this weekend instead?

Lesson B We've got to get going.

1 Building vocabulary and grammar

A Listen. Where are Luis and Rosa going? Do they want to go? Practice the conversation.

Luis Rosa, it's 6:00. We're supposed to be there by 7:00. Weren't you supposed to **get off** work early today?

Rosa Well, my boss called a meeting, and I couldn't **get out of** it. I had to go. Anyway, I don't **get it** – why is your cousin getting married on a Friday and not a Saturday, like everyone else?

Luis I don't know. All I know is that my mother will never **get over** it if we walk in late. So we have to **get going**.

Rosa OK. Uh, do you think I can **get away with** wearing pants?

Luis No way! It's supposed to be a formal wedding. Look, I got your silk dress ready for you.

Rosa Oh, I'll never **get used to** dressing up for these fancy weddings. Can we try to **get home** early?

Luis Rosa, I **get the feeling** that you don't really want to go.

Rosa Well, I just hope I can **get through** the reception.

Luis Oh, come on. Let's just go and enjoy it. It's a chance for you to **get to know** my family better. By the way, did you **get around to** buying a gift?

Rosa Weren't *you* supposed to do that?

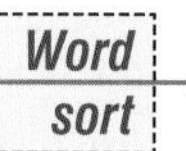

B Find a *get* expression from the conversation above to complete each example sentence below. Are the sentences true for you? Compare with a partner.

get expression	Example sentences
1. get off	*I usually get off work early on Fridays. I leave at about 3:00.*
2. ________	*I don't like to stay at work late. I always try to ________ by 5:30 to cook dinner.*
3. ________	*I was so busy last week that I didn't ________ doing my homework.*
4. ________	*I'm usually late, so my friends are always saying, "We have to ________."*
5. ________	*Sometimes I ________ that people are annoyed with me for being late.*
6. ________	*I like going out after class. It's a chance to ________ my classmates.*
7. ________	*It's hard for me to finish long novels. I just can't ________ them.*
8. ________	*I don't know why people dress up for weddings. I just don't ________.*
9. ________	*I'll never ________ wearing formal clothes. They don't feel right.*
10. ________	*I wish I could ________ wearing jeans all the time. They're so comfortable.*

Figure it out

C Can you put the words in the right order to complete the sentences? Compare with a partner.

1. Rosa had to attend a meeting at work. She couldn't ________ (out / it / get / of).
2. Luis's mother will be upset if they're late. She'll never ________ (it / over / get).

2 Grammar *Inseparable phrasal verbs*

With these verbs, the object always comes after the particle or preposition.

Verb + particle + object

Weren't you supposed to **get off** work early?

She'll never **get over** feeling embarrassed.
  I'm sure she'll **get over** it.

I hope I can **get through** the reception.
  I know you can **get through** it.

Verb + particle + preposition + object

Can I **get away with** wearing pants?
  No. You can't **get away with** it.

Couldn't you **get out of** the meeting?
  No, I couldn't **get out of** it.

Did you **get around to** buying a gift?
  No, I never **got around to** it.

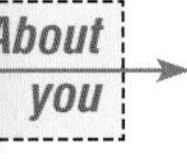

Complete the questions. Put the words in order, and use the correct form of the verbs. Then ask and answer the questions with a partner.

1. If you had an important date, would you try to ________ (get / of / come / out) to class? Would you ask if you could ________ (off / work / get) early?
2. Do you find it hard to ________ (the week / through / get) if you don't have time to go out with friends?
3. Do you have any shy friends who are always trying to ________ (of / get / go / out) to parties? What can they do to ________ (get / their shyness / over)?
4. Have you ever told a "white lie" to ________ (of / get / an invitation / out)? Did you ________ (get / it / away / with)?
5. How quickly can you ________ (through / get / your e-mail)? Does it take you a long time to ________ (answer / to / get / around) e-mail from friends?
6. How do you feel about buying gifts? Does it take you a long time to ________ (to / get / it / around)?

3 Speaking and listening *What are you like?*

A Look at the sentences below. Which choice is most like you? Tell a partner.

1. I'm one of those people who ...
   a. gets ready at the last minute.
   b. spends ages getting ready.
2. If I'm late for something, I usually ...
   a. hurry to try to be on time.
   b. take my time and arrive late.
3. When I go out, I always ...
   a. make an effort to dress up.
   b. try and get away with wearing jeans.
4. If a friend cancels plans we made, ...
   a. I stay home and feel disappointed.
   b. I get over it and do something else instead.

B Listen to Paula and Roberto talk about their plans for tonight. What happens?

C Listen again. How would Roberto complete the sentences above? Circle his choices.

4 Vocabulary notebook *Get this!*

See page 42 for a useful way to log and learn vocabulary.

Lesson C So, it's your birthday?

1 Conversation strategy *Checking your understanding*

A How are the two questions in this conversation different?

A	***So, um, are you going out tonight?***	*A*	***You're going out with Karl?***
B	***Yes, I'll probably meet Karl.***	*B*	***Yeah.***

Now listen. What does Martin usually do on his birthday?

Grant **So, it's your birthday Friday, right?**

Martin **Yeah, but I've never made a big deal about it. It's been a long time since I've had a party or anything.**

Grant **What if somebody planned a surprise party?**

Martin **One time my wife did. We were talking and I said, "You know, this year for my birthday, let's just hang out, rent a movie." And she got really quiet.**

Grant **Oh, really? When you said that?**

Martin **Yeah. Then she said, "I invited all your old friends over." And I said, "Well, they're my old friends for a reason." It was a disaster.**

Grant **So they all came, huh?**

Martin **Yeah. They all came, so . . .**

Notice **how Grant checks his understanding. He asks questions in the form of statements. People often add *huh* or *right* at the end of questions like these. Find more examples.**

"So, it's your birthday Friday, right?"

B Read more of their conversation. Change Grant's questions to "statement questions." Then listen and notice what Grant actually says.

Grant So, was it supposed to be a surprise? 1. So, it was supposed to be a surprise?
And did you know about it? 2. you knew about it.
Martin Yeah. I already knew.
Grant Was the party the next day? 3. The party was the next day.
Martin No, it was probably like a week later.
Grant Oh, so did you have a week to feel bad about it? 4. So, you had a week to feel bad about it.
Martin Yeah. I had a whole week to think about it.
Grant So did you really hate the party? 5. So you really hated the party.
Martin Well, kind of. I mean, it was really sweet of her to do that, but . . .

SELF-STUDY AUDIO CD CD-ROM

2 Strategy plus *so*

You can use *so* in many ways, including:

To start a topic, often with a question
So, it's your birthday Friday, right?

To check your understanding
So they all came, huh?

To pause or let the other person draw a conclusion
They all came, so . . .

To close a topic
So that's what happened. They all came.

A Find three places where you can use *so* in each conversation. Change the capital letters and add commas where necessary. Then practice with a partner.

In conversation . . .

So is one of the top 20 words.

1. *A* ___ What do you think of surprise parties?
   B ___ I don't know. I've never had one or been to one.
   A ___ No one ever gave you one? Do you think your friends would ever do that?
   B ___ No. My friends don't do that kind of thing. ___ Probably not.
2. *A* ___ Has anyone ever given you a gift as a surprise, for no reason?
   B ___ Actually, yes. My friend gave me this great book. ___ I didn't expect it.
   A ___ It wasn't for your birthday or anything?
   B ___ No, she just gave it to me because she wanted to, ___ . . .
3. *A* ___ Have you been to any good parties lately?
   B ___ Well, I've been very busy at work recently, ___ . . .
   A ___ You haven't been going out too often, then?
   B ___ No, I guess not.

About you → **B** ***Pair work*** Ask and answer the questions. Give your own answers.

3 Speaking naturally *Being sure or checking*

If you are sure: *So your birthday's on Friday.*
So all your friends came.

If you are checking: *So your birthday's on Friday?*
So all your friends came?

A Listen and repeat the sentences. Notice how the intonation falls when you say something you are sure about, and rises when you're checking information.

B Listen to four conversations. Are the speakers sure, or are they checking? Add a period or a question mark, and write ***S*** or ***C***.

1. So you go out a lot ___
2. So you're a real people person ___
3. So you don't like parties very much ___
4. So you never celebrate your birthday ___

Lesson D Social style

1 Reading

A Are you an extrovert? Do you enjoy socializing and meeting new people? Or are you more of an introvert, someone who prefers to spend time alone? Tell the class.

B Read the article. What's Marti Olsen Laney's book about?

Socializing the introvert

A confirmed introvert says it's OK to be that way. She should know. She's a psychologist who has written a book on the subject. *By Jenny Yuen*

As an introvert, Marti Olsen Laney knows how difficult it can be to socialize. She sometimes heads straight for the bathroom the second she arrives at a party. But she's not exactly paralyzed in a crowd. In fact, the California psychologist seemed entirely at ease last week as she addressed about 20 people who turned out for her discussion of the introverted personality. Perhaps predictably, those in the audience did not sit close to each other. But that's OK. Really. The author of *Introvert Advantage* revealed that being introverted is quite normal. "We've all grown up in an extroverted society," Olsen Laney said. "There really is quite a concept of negativity attached to introverts."

Thinking outside the box

Many people prefer to spend time alone, work better independently than in group settings, and cherish celebrating birthdays with close friends rather than with large groups. This introverted personality is often stereotyped as unstable, lonely, and antisocial, but Olsen Laney said there are many advantages to being introverted.

She said introverts are likely to be resilient, determined, good listeners, creative thinkers, and very knowledgeable about themselves. "Introverts think outside the box. They also express themselves better in writing than in speech," Olsen Laney said.

Behavior often mistaken for aloofness

Introversion may affect one's family life if there is a clash of extroverted parents with introverted kids. It may also impact one's career if a boss does not think an introverted employee contributes enough, because introverts tend to keep information to themselves. This behavior is often mistaken for aloofness.

"If you just ask them, it's amazing what ideas they'll tell you," she said.

Still, Olsen Laney said there are ways for introverts to cope with uncomfortable social functions without mentally breaking down. She said they can be social at events where there is interesting conversation, but not when it's a party that they feel is meaningless.

"Introverted people don't like to be interrupted because it's hard to find your train of thought again," she said. "A lot of the reasons introverted people are seen the way they are is because chitchat is totally unrewarding for our system."

Being introverted in an extroverted world

Olsen Laney recommended that introverts restore body energy by taking breaks and spending quiet time alone to shut out extra stimuli so they don't become overwhelmed or feel the need to change themselves.

"All introverts have to be extroverted in their life without having to change completely," she said. "It's important to find the balance of having an occupation where you can be extroverted and still have time for yourself."

Source: *Toronto Observer*

C Can you find words or expressions in the article that mean these things? Underline them.

1. unable to move or speak
2. thinking creatively
3. able to get over things easily
4. unfriendliness
5. a conflict between
6. have an effect on
7. remember what you were thinking
8. small talk

D Read the article again, and answer the questions. Then compare your answers with a partner.

1. Is Marti Olsen Laney an extrovert or an introvert?
2. How do introverts generally feel about working or socializing in groups?
3. What are some good qualities that introverts can have?
4. What are some problems that introverts encounter in society?
5. Why are introverted people often not comfortable at parties?
6. How does Marti Olsen Laney advise introverts to cope with life in an extroverted society?

2 Listening and writing *Extrovert or introvert?*

About you

A ***Group work*** Take the magazine quiz, and discuss the questions. How are you the same?

What's your social style?

Do you prefer to . . .

	EXTROVERT	INTROVERT	ANSWERS Me		ANSWERS Jun	
1.	a. go out and socialize?	b. see friends at home?	a	b	a	b
2.	a. have lots of friends?	b. have just a few close friends?	a	b	a	b
3.	a. go out in a big group?	b. go out with one or two friends?	a	b	a	b
4.	a. be the center of attention?	b. keep a low profile?	a	b	a	b
5.	a. tell jokes and stories?	b. listen as other people tell jokes?	a	b	a	b
6.	a. engage in chitchat?	b. have more serious conversations?	a	b	a	b
7.	a. do tasks with others?	b. figure things out alone?	a	b	a	b
8.	a. think of yourself as a "social animal"?	b. think of yourself as an individual?	a	b	a	b

B Listen to Jun talk about his social life. How would he answer the quiz? Circle his answers.

C Write a short article about your social style. Are you an introvert, an extrovert, or a little of both?

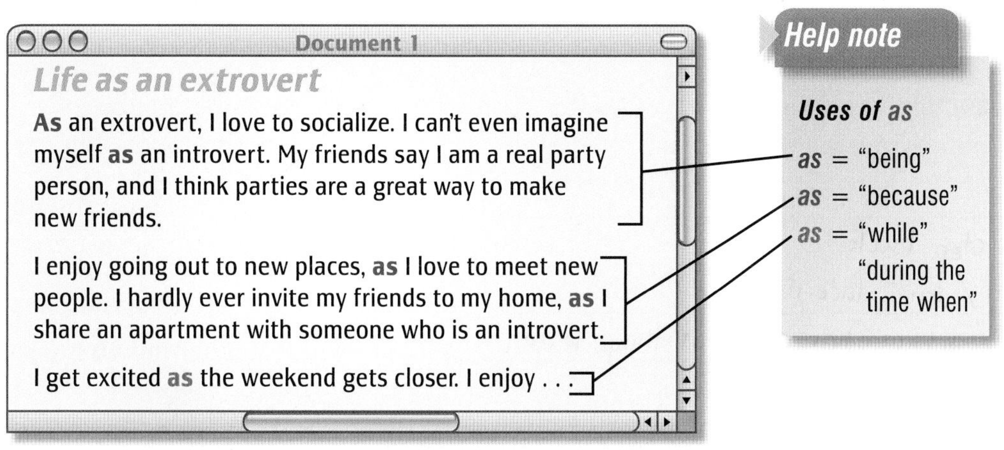
Document 1

Life as an extrovert

As an extrovert, I love to socialize. I can't even imagine myself **as** an introvert. My friends say I am a real party person, and I think parties are a great way to make new friends.

I enjoy going out to new places, **as** I love to meet new people. I hardly ever invite my friends to my home, **as** I share an apartment with someone who is an introvert.

I get excited **as** the weekend gets closer. I enjoy . . .

Help note

Uses of as

as = "being"
as = "because"
as = "while" "during the time when"

D ***Group work*** Read your classmates' articles. Have they supported their points with clear examples? Can you offer suggestions to improve their writing?

3 Free talk *Pass on the message.*

See ***Free talk 4*** for more speaking practice.

Vocabulary notebook

Get this!

Learning tip *Expressions in context*

When you learn a new expression, write an example sentence that uses it in context. Think of something you might want to say, and add ideas that set the scene or help you remember its meaning.

Get into it!

The top 10 particles and prepositions after ***get*** are:

1. out	6. up
2. into	7. on
3. in	8. away
4. to	9. off
5. back	10. down

1 Complete the sentences using a *get* expression from the box.

get away with it	get it	get out of it	get to know
get going	get off	get over it	get used to

1. I'm late. I'd better __get going__ .
2. I love meeting new people. I think it's a lot of fun to __get to know__ people.
3. Weekends seem so short. I wish I could __get off__ work early every Friday.
4. You're not supposed to go into clubs under the age of 18, but I know some kids manage to __get away with it__.
5. I'll never __get used to__ wearing a suit to work.
6. I don't understand why some people stay home all the time. I just don't __get it__ .
7. I was going to go to my class reunion. But I've decided to try and __get out of it__ .
8. When I failed the exam, I thought I would never __get over it__ , but actually, I'm enjoying taking this class again.

2 *Word builder* Find out the meaning of the *get* expressions in the sentences below. Then write another sentence before each one that provides a context for the expression.

1. ______________________ She **gets on my nerves.**
2. __take a step back__ I just need to **get away from it all** so I can relax.
3. __avoid / don't face it__ Maybe there's a way to **get around** that problem.
4. __~~take~~?! like : have a lot of things to do__ I don't want to **get behind on** my payments.

On your own

Get a flip pad. Make different sections for common verbs like *get*, *go*, *do*, and *have*. Write as many expressions as you can for each verb.

Unit 5

Law and order

In Unit 5, you learn how to . . .

- use the passive of modal verbs.
- use the *get* passive.
- talk about rules and regulations, crime and punishment.
- organize your views with expressions like *First of all, Basically,* etc.
- use expressions like *That's a good point* to show someone has a valid argument.

1

2

3

Before you begin . . .

Do you have laws about these things in your country? What are they?

- wearing seat belts and using a cell phone in a car
- at what age you can ride a motorcycle and what you have to wear
- how you should get rid of litter or garbage

Lesson A Rules and regulations

The Age of **Majority**

In many countries, the law permits you to engage in new activities at the age of 18. We asked people what they think about 18 as the "age of majority."

When you turn 18, you can go see an "R-rated" movie – a movie that's restricted to adults. What do you think about that?

"What do I think? Well, I think the law ought to be changed – 18 is too young. Actually, I think R-rated movies should be banned altogether. They're far too violent."

– Bill Hughes

Do you think you should be able to get married before you're 18?

"No way. In fact, you shouldn't be allowed to get married until you're at least 21 or even older. Then there might be fewer divorces. Actually, I think a law should be passed that says if you want to get married, you have to take marriage classes first!"

– Maya Diaz

Do you think you should be allowed to vote at 18?

"I guess. I mean, you can do everything else at 18. Why not vote? It's too bad more young people don't vote, though. I think everyone should be made to vote."

– Aiko Niwano

You can get your own credit card at the age of 18. Is this too young?

"I don't think so. I mean, young people have to be given their freedom at some point. You know, they ought to be encouraged to manage their own finances and things. They can always learn from their mistakes."

– Jared Blake

The legal age for most things is 18, but in many places you can drive at 16. Is that a good idea, do you think?

"I must say I've always thought 16 is too young. Too many teenagers get involved in traffic accidents, and something really must be done about it. The legal age for driving could easily be changed to 18 or 21 or something like that."

– Pat Johnson

1 Getting started

A Listen to these interviews. What five things do the people talk about? Do they think 18 is the right age to start doing these things? What are the laws in your country?

Figure it out

B How do the people above say these things? Find the sentences in the article, and underline them. Do you agree with these views? Discuss with a partner.

1. They should ban R-rated movies.
2. They shouldn't allow you to get married until you're 21.
3. They should make everyone vote.
4. They ought to encourage young people to manage their own finances.
5. They could easily change the legal age for driving to 18.

2 Grammar *The passive of modal verbs*

Modal verb + be + past participle

R-rated movies **should be banned**.
You **shouldn't be allowed** to marry at 18.
They **have to be given** their freedom.
The legal age **could** easily **be changed**.
Something **must be done** about it.
The law **ought to be changed**.

In conversation . . .

Must means "have to" in 10% of its uses. In this meaning, it is often used in expressions like ***I must admit*** and ***I must say***.

90% of the uses of ***must*** are for speculation:

Things must be hard for couples who marry young.

A Read these views about different laws. Rewrite the sentences starting with the words given.

1. They must do something about junk e-mail. Something . . .
   Something must be done about junk e-mail.
2. They ought to arrest people for sending spam. People . . . ought to be arrested
3. They have to do something about all the litter on the buses and in subways. Something . . . has to be / must be done
4. They shouldn't allow people to eat food on public transportation. People . . . shouldn't be allowed
5. They ought to fine people for making noise after midnight. People . . . ought to be fined
6. They shouldn't allow people to buy fireworks. People . . . shouldn't be allowed
7. They should ban all movies with violent scenes. All movies . . . should be banned
8. They could encourage people to stop smoking if there were more anti-smoking laws. People . . . could be encouraged
9. They could easily ban smoking in all public places – nobody would complain. Smoking . . . could easily be banned
10. They shouldn't allow children to quit school until they are 18. Children . . . shouldn't be allowed. . .

About you → **B *Pair work*** Discuss the sentences with a partner. Which statements do you agree with?

A ***I agree that something must be done about junk e-mail.***
B ***Absolutely. I think spam ought to be totally banned. It wastes too much time.***

3 Speaking naturally *Saying conversational expressions*

I mean**, you can do everything else at 18. Why not vote? **You know what I mean?
***You know**, they ought to be encouraged to manage their own finances **and things**.* = and such
*The legal age for driving could easily be changed to 18 or 21 **or something like that**.*

A Listen and repeat the sentences above. Notice how the expressions in bold are said more quickly, even when the speaker is speaking slowly.

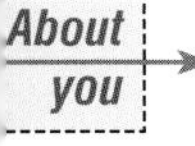

B *Group work* Discuss the questions in the interviews on page 44. Then decide on . . .

- three laws that should be passed.
- three things that people should be encouraged to do.
- three things that people ought to be allowed to do.

Lesson B Crime and punishment

What punishment best fits the crime?

Here are some opinions from readers of *The Daily Gazette*.

1 "I think **shoplifters** should be **fined** at first, but if they get caught **stealing** again and again, they should go to **jail**."

2 "I don't know. Some people get **sentenced** to only 10 or 15 years for **murder**. **Killing** another person is the worst crime, but it's a complex issue."

3 "That depends. If you commit **armed robbery**, you know, use a **gun** or a **knife**, you should be sent to prison."

4 "**Taking** someone **captive** and asking for money is a major crime. **Kidnappers** should go to prison for a long time."

5 "If the **vandalism** isn't too serious, they should just have to clean up their **graffiti**, or pay for any damage."

6 "**Breaking into** someone's home is serious. But first-time **burglars** should just be **put on probation**."

7 "You don't usually get **arrested** for speeding unless you cause an accident, and that seems fair. But if you get stopped a lot, you should **lose your license**."

8 "A **fine**, maybe? I know it's **against the law** to just cross the street anywhere, but it's relatively minor **offense**. And the law doesn't get **enforced** much."

1 Building vocabulary and grammar

A Read the opinions from readers in the newspaper above. What questions are they answering? Number the questions below. Then listen and check your answers.

8 What's the right **penalty** for **jaywalking**?

7 Should they **arrest** drivers who get caught **speeding**?

1 What should happen if you get caught **shoplifting** from a store?

5 How should **vandals** be **punished**?

3 What punishment should you get for **robbing** someone?

6 What should happen to someone who is **convicted** of **burglary**?

4 What kind of **sentence** should you get for **kidnapping**?

2 Should all **murderers** be sentenced to **life in prison**?

Word sort → **B** Complete the chart. Then describe each crime or offense to a partner. Which do you think are major crimes? Which are minor offenses?

crime / offense	shoplifting	jaywalking	vandalism		burglary		murder
person	shoplifter	jaywalker	vandal	robber	burgla	kidnapper	

"Shoplifting is when you steal things from a store. I think it's a relatively minor offense."

Figure it out → **C** What happens to people in your country when they break the law? Complete the sentences with expressions from the article. Then compare with a partner.

1. People who commit murder usually get ______________________ .
2. If you get caught shoplifting, you usually get ______________________ .
3. If a person commits burglary for the first time, he or she gets ______________________ .

2 Grammar *get passive vs. be passive*

Examples of *get* passive
People who speed don't usually **get arrested**.
Some murderers **get sentenced** to only 10 years.

After should, the be passive is more common.
People who speed should **be arrested** if they cause an accident.
Some murderers should **be sentenced** to life in prison.

Notice:
catch + verb + -ing
What happens if they **catch** you **shoplifting**?
What happens if you get **caught shoplifting**?

In conversation . . .
People use the ***get*** passive much more frequently in speaking than in writing.

A Complete the comments about law enforcement. Use the *get* passive or *be* passive with the verb given.

1. "Vandalism should _be punished_ (punish) more severely. Vandals should _be sentenced_ (sentence) to a month of community service."
2. "More shoplifters _get caught_ (catch) these days because of all the cameras they have in stores. Just the same, most shoppers are honest, and they really shouldn't _be videotaped_ (videotape)."
3. "People who speed hardly ever _get stopped_ (stop) by the police. The laws against speeding should _be enforced_ (enforce) more strictly."
4. "Lots of executives _get caught_ (catch) stealing from their companies, but they _don't get sent_ (not send) to prison for very long. It doesn't seem right."
5. "A big problem is that most criminals never _get caught_ (catch), and the ones that _get arrested_ (arrest) often _don't get convicted_ (not convict)."
6. "People under 18 shouldn't _be given_ (give) a prison sentence if they commit a crime. They should just _be put_ (put) on probation."

About you → **B *Pair work*** Discuss the statements and opinions above. Do you agree?

C *Group work* Discuss the questions from Exercise 1A on page 46. Do you all agree?

3 Listening *We got robbed!*

A Listen to Jenny talk about a burglary. Answer the questions.

1. When did the burglary happen? couple years ago
2. Who discovered it and how? the neighbor
3. What did the burglars take? 2 computers
4. Did the burglars get caught? She doesn't think so.

B Listen again. How does Jenny feel about the burglary? Check (✓) the sentences.

- [x] She never expected it to happen.
- [ ] She was scared.
- [ ] She thinks it was funny.
- [x] She feels she was luckier than many people.
- [ ] She was very angry and upset.
- [ ] She thinks it was inconvenient.

4 Vocabulary notebook *It's a crime!*

See page 52 for a new way to log and learn vocabulary.

Lesson C Well, basically . . .

1 Conversation strategy *Organizing your views*

A **Imagine you are giving your views about something. In what order could you use these expressions to organize what you say?**

____ *Second* ____ *Another thing is* ____ *First of all*

Now listen. What do Jin Ho and Celia think of security cameras?

Jin Ho *What do you think of all these security cameras they have now?*

Celia *Well, basically I'm in favor of them.*

Jin Ho *You are?*

Celia *Yeah. I mean, for two reasons. First, they're like a deterrent – you're not go. to commit a crime if you know you're being filmed on camera, and secondly, they help the police catch criminals.*

Jin Ho *Well, that's true. But on the other hand don't you think they're a bit intrusive?*

Celia *But if you're not doing anything wrong, what's the problem?*

Jin Ho *Well, that's a good point, but some pec would say it's an invasion of privacy – someone watching you all the time.*

Celia *I guess. I must admit, I never thought of it that way.*

Notice **how Celia organizes what she says by using expressions like these. Find the ones she uses.**

Giving main ideas:	*Basically . . . The point / thing is . . .*
Adding ideas:	*Another thing is . . .*
Introducing a list:	*There are two problems. . . . . . . for two reasons.*
Ordinal numbers:	*First (of all), . . . Second (of all), / Secondly, . . .*
Numbers or letters:	*(Number) One, . . . Two, . . .* **or** *A, . . . B, . . .*

B ***Pair work*** Have a conversation about security cameras like the one above. Use these ideas or your own, and organize what you say. Take turns arguing for and against.

For security cameras	**Against security cameras**
They help reduce crime rates.	They're intrusive.
They help the police solve crimes.	They're an invasion of privacy.
They make people feel safer.	They're expensive. They're a waste of money.

A ***Do you think there should be security cameras everywhere?***

B ***Well, basically I think it's a good idea to have them. I mean, for two reasons. First, . . .***

2 Strategy plus *That's a good point.*

You can use *That's a good point* and other expressions like these to show someone has a valid argument – even if you don't completely agree:

That's true.
You've got a point (there).
I never (really) thought of it that way.

They help the police.
That's true.

In conversation . . .

That's true is the second most common expression with ***That's***, after ***That's right***.

A Write a response to these points of view, using one of the expressions above and adding a different or an opposing view.

1. People who speed should lose their licenses, I think. Speeding causes so many accidents.
   That's true, but I think they should also be made to take more driving lessons.
2. I think they should use metal detectors in all public buildings. That way people wouldn't carry knives with them.
3. They should punish the parents of kids who skip school. It's the parents who should be responsible.
4. I don't think people should have to carry ID cards. I mean, what are you supposed to do if you go to the beach?
5. They should raise the legal age for driving to 20. There would be fewer accidents.

B *Pair work* Take turns presenting the views above and the other views that you wrote. Continue your arguments.

3 Listening and speaking *Different points of view*

A Listen to the class debate. Answer the questions.

1. Which of these topics is the class discussing? Check (✓) the topic.

- [ ] Raising the age limit to get married
- [ ] Sending dangerous drivers to prison
- [ ] Banning cars from city areas
- [x] Raising the legal age for driving

2. What two arguments are given in favor of changing the law? Take notes.
3. What two arguments are given against changing the law? Take notes.

About you

B Listen to these opinions from the debate again. Prepare a response to each point of view. Use an expression from the box, and add your own opinion.

1. ______________________
2. ______________________
3. ______________________
4. ______________________
5. ______________________

Useful expressions

That's a good point, but . . .
Absolutely! I agree with that.
Maybe, but on the other hand, . . .
That's a good idea.
I'm not sure about that for two reasons.

C *Group work* Discuss one of the topics in part A, item 1. Do you share the same views?

Lesson D Your rights

1 Reading

A Do you or any of your friends have a cam phone? What can you use a cam phone for? Are there any places where you're not allowed to use one? Why?

B Read the article. What is it about? Choose one of the ideas.

a. People using cell phones at work
b. People taking pictures for the wrong reasons
c. The advantages of cam phones

CAM PHONES, GO HOME!

by Carolina A. Miranda

Those camera-equipped cell phones may be the latest must-have tech product, with more than 31 million sold in North America last year alone. But the ability of users to snap pictures on the sly almost anywhere they go – and even put images on the Internet – has prompted a growing number of places to institute a ban on the devices.

Several large companies – even one of the leading producers of the phones – are among the companies that have prohibited employees from taking cam phones into sensitive research and production facilities, to prevent corporate espionage. Schools are banning them to halt cheating, since students have been nabbed shooting test questions and e-mailing them to others. Many courthouses ban the phones to prevent witness or juror intimidation. (At a superior court hearing, a witness was photographed by a cam-phone user who threatened to post the photo on the Web.) Most gyms have set limits, especially in locker rooms, fearing members could take pictures of people in various states of undress.

Those localized bans, however, do little for anyone in a public area. One popular Web site proudly touts photos shot by cam phones in malls and parking lots. "People need to be aware that whatever you do in a public space can be recorded," says attorney Kevin Bankston of the Electronic Frontier Foundation, an online civil-liberties group.

C Find expressions in the article to complete the sentences below.

1. Everyone wants a cam phone. They've become a ______ tech product.
2. With a cam phone, you can take pictures ______ – without anyone knowing.
3. There are sometimes spies in a company that use cam phones for ______.
4. Criminals sometimes scare or threaten jurors or witnesses. That's called ______.
5. Cam phones are often banned in specific locations, but these ______ don't protect people in public places.
6. One Web site boldly advertises cam-phone photos. They ______ the photos proudly.
7. There's a ______ group that helps protect people's privacy and freedom online.

D Find these verbs in the article. Can you guess their meaning from context?

snap	**institute**	**prevent**	**nabbed**
prompted	**prohibited**	**halt**	**shooting**

E Read the article again, and find . . .

1. what happens to many of the photographs that people take with cam phones.
2. four places that have banned cam phones and why.
3. why people need to be careful about what they do in public.

2 Speaking and writing *Letters to the editor . . .*

About you

A ***Pair work*** What do you think about the magazine article on page 50? Discuss the questions.

1. Do you think the topic of the article is relevant?
2. Are you concerned about the issues it raises?
3. Have you ever seen anyone use a cam phone inappropriately?
4. What should be done to prevent people from misusing cam phones?

B Write a letter to the editor of the magazine, responding to the article. Use the ideas from your discussion above to state your views.

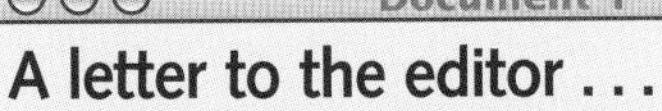

A letter to the editor . . .

I was interested to read your recent article on cam phones. I think the problems it talked about are very relevant here, **as** so many people now use them.

I think the biggest problem is cheating in schools, **since** students can use their phones to take photos of test questions and then send them to other students.

I have never used a cam phone, **because** I would rather use my digital camera to take photos.

Help note

Giving reasons

- You can use ***because***, ***since***, and ***as*** to give reasons.
  *Cam phones should be banned in schools, **because** / **since** / **as** they can be misused by students.*
- You can use ***because*** in all cases. Use ***since*** only to give reasons that the reader already knows or can guess. ***As*** is more formal.

C Post your letters around the classroom. Read your classmates' letters. Find someone who raises an issue you hadn't thought about.

3 Free talk *Lawmakers*

See ***Free talk 5*** for more speaking practice.

Vocabulary notebook

It's a crime!

Learning tip Word charts

One way to write down new words is to use word charts. You can group related ideas together, which will help you learn and remember them.

Get paid, not fired!

In conversation, the top 6 ***get*** passive verbs are:

1. get ***paid***
2. get ***caught***
3. get ***hurt***
4. get ***killed***
5. get ***elected***
6. get ***fired***

1 Complete the word chart about crime using the words and expressions in the box.

burglar	murderer	steals from stores	paints on public buildings
murder	shoplifting	vandalism	breaks into a building to steal

Crime	*Criminal*	*Activity*
burglary	burglar	stealing from a home or store or any places that you don't know
vandalism	*vandal*	paint / break public stuffs
murder	murderer	*kills or murders people*
shoplifting	*shoplifter*	stealing from a store or shop

2 ***Word builder*** Find out the meaning of the crime words in this chart. Then complete the chart, adding more words and definitions.

Crime	*Criminal*	*Activity*
arson	arsonist	
blackmail	blackmailer	destroy reputation
hijacking	hijacker	
joyriding	joyrider	
mugging	mugger	

On your own

Look through an English-language newspaper, and highlight all the words that are connected with crime and law. How many of them do you already know?

Unit 6

Strange events

In Unit 6, you learn how to . . .

- use the past perfect.
- use responses with *So* and *Neither*.
- talk about coincidences, superstitions, and strange events.
- repeat your ideas to make your meaning clear.
- use *just* to make what you say stronger or softer.

2 When you can tell what someone else is thinking, you are experiencing ________.

1 When you have the strange feeling that you have been somewhere or experienced something before, you are having ________.

4 When you unexpectedly run into someone you know – for example, in another city – you call it ________.

3 When you see an unexplained object in the sky, you might be seeing ________.

Before you begin . . .

Complete the sentences with the words below.

- telepathy
- a coincidence
- déjà vu
- a UFO (unidentified flying object)

Have you ever had an experience like these?
Do you know anyone else who has?

Lesson A Coincidences

Have you ever experienced an *amazing coincidence?*

"Actually, yeah. One thing that sticks in my mind is . . . years ago, I was out in the Australian outback, driving through the desert. One night, I had set up camp and was cooking, and this van appeared out of nowhere with two guys in it. It was nice to have company because I hadn't spoken to anyone in days – I'd gone on this trip by myself, you see. Well, it turned out one of them had graduated from the same college I did. Small world, huh?"

– **Glen Hutt**

"Oh, yeah, I think life is full of coincidences. I remember one time – I had just met my husband-to-be, and we hadn't known each other long. Well, he was showing me photos of an old friend that he hadn't seen or spoken to in years, a college friend who'd moved to Spain. Gerry. Anyway, there we were, looking at these photos when the phone rang, and – you'll never believe it – it was his friend Gerry! He just called out of the blue."

– **Emma Rivers**

1 Getting started

A Listen. What coincidences did these people experience?

Figure it out → **B** Complete the answers. Look at the anecdotes to help you.

1. Why was Glen happy to have company? Because he ________ to anyone in days.
2. Why wasn't Glen with his friends? Because he ________ on the trip by himself.
3. Were Emma's husband and Gerry close? Yes, but they ________ to each other in years.
4. What did Emma find out about Gerry? He ________ to Spain years ago.

2 Grammar *The past perfect*

Use the past perfect to talk about things that happened before an event in the past.

I **had set up** camp and was cooking, and this van appeared out of nowhere.

I **had** just **met** my husband-to-be, and he was showing me photos . . . when the phone rang.

The past perfect is often used to give explanations or reasons why things happened.

It was nice to have company because I **hadn't spoken** to anyone in days.

Gerry was a college friend that he **hadn't seen** in years. He**'d moved** to Spain.

Questions and short answers in the past perfect

Had you **gone** by yourself?	**Had** they **been** in touch?	Where **had** he **moved to**?
Yes, I had.	No, they hadn't.	To Spain.

A Complete the stories with either the simple past or past perfect. Sometimes both are possible. Then practice with a partner.

1. *A* Have you ever been talking about someone, and then they called you?
   B Yeah. That happens to me a lot. In fact, last week I was thinking about a friend who I __hadn't called__ (not call) in ages. I think I ~~had thrown~~ threw (throw away) his phone number by accident, and we __hadn't been__ (not be) in touch for months. Anyway, he __called__ (call) me out of the blue. It turned out that he __had lost__ (lose) my number, too, but then he __found__ (find) it.
2. *A* Have you ever run into someone you were thinking about?
   B No, I haven't, but I've experienced other coincidences. For example, one time a friend of mine __called__ (call) me because she __had left__ (leave) her purse on the subway. She __didn't know__ (not know) what to do. And right then, my sister __came__ (come) home with a purse that she __had found__ (find) on the subway, and guess what? It __was__ (be) my friend's purse!
3. *A* Have you ever met anyone with the same birthday as you?
   B Yes, my friend Tom. The funny thing is, last year I __decided__ (decide) to buy him something special because he __had helped__ (help) me fix my car many times. So I __got__ (get) him this camera that we __had seen__ (see) when we were out shopping the week before. When we __opened__ (open) our presents, we __laughed__ (laugh). We __had bought__ (buy) each other exactly the same thing!

About you → **B** ***Pair work*** Ask and answer the questions. Tell your own stories.

3 Listening *It's a small world!*

Listen to Jody tell a friend about a coincidence. Answer the questions.

1. How did Jody and Janeen first get to know each other? They were roommate in
2. How long have they been friends now? 10 years
3. How long had they been out of touch when they met up again? 3-4 years
4. Where did they both end up living? in New york.
5. How did they try to get in touch again?
6. What coincidence makes both speakers say "small world"?
   They are working and leaving very close. (in the same buildi

Lesson B Superstitions

Superstitions from around the World

Taiwan If you see a crow in the morning, you will have a bad day.

Japan It's lucky to find a tea leaf floating upright in a cup of green tea.

Thailand Dream of a snake holding you tightly, and you will soon meet your soul mate.

Brazil If you leave your purse on the floor, your money will disappear.

Venezuela If someone sweeps over an unmarried woman's feet with a broom, she'll never get married.

South Korea If you give a boyfriend or girlfriend a pair of shoes, he or she will leave you.

Argentina Pick up any coins you find, and you'll soon come into money.

Peru If you put clothes on inside out, you will get a nice surprise.

Mexico If a bride wears pearls, she will cry all her married life.

Turkey Your wish will come true if you stand between two people with the same name.

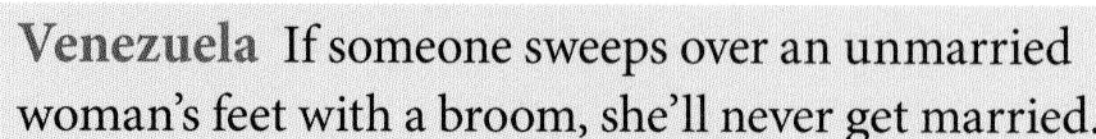

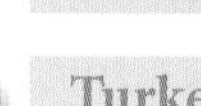

1 Building vocabulary

A Read the superstitions above. How many have you heard of? Do you have any similar superstitions in your country?

Word sort → **B** Complete the chart with the superstitions above. Add ideas. Then compare with a partner.

It's good luck to . . .	*It's bad luck to . . .*
find a green tea leaf floating upright.	leave your purse on the floor.

2 Speaking and listening *Lucky or not?*

A Do you know any superstitions about the things below? Tell the class.

1 

2 

3 

4 

B Listen to four people talk about superstitions. Do they think the things above are lucky (**L**) or unlucky (**U**)? Write ***L*** or ***U*** in the boxes.

C Listen again. Can you write down each superstition? Compare with a partner.

3 Building language

A Listen. Is Angie superstitious? How about Terry? Practice the conversation.

Angie Gosh, this looks good. I'm so hungry.
Terry So am I. Could you pass the salt?
Angie Sure. . . . Whoops! You know, it's supposed to be unlucky to spill salt.
Terry It is? I didn't know that.
Angie No, neither did I, until I read it on the Internet.
Terry Actually, I don't believe in all that superstitious stuff.
Angie Oh, I do. Now I always throw a pinch of salt over my shoulder if I spill it. And I never put shoes on the table.
Terry Well, neither do I. But that's because they're dirty.
Angie And I always walk around a ladder – never under it.
Terry Oh, so do I. But that's so nothing falls on my head!

B Underline two expressions above that mean *Me neither*, and two that mean *Me too*.

4 Grammar *Responses with So and Neither*

I'**m** hungry.	I'**m not** very superstitious.
So am I. (I am too.)	**Neither am** I. (I'm not either.)
I always **walk** around ladders.	I **didn't know** it was unlucky to spill salt.
So do I. (I do too.)	**Neither did** I. (I didn't either.)

A Respond to each of these statements with *So* or *Neither*. Then practice with a partner.

1. I think it's silly to be superstitious. So do I.
2. I don't know anyone who is superstitious.
3. I didn't know the superstition about spilling salt.
4. I walk under ladders all the time.
5. I'm usually a very lucky person.
6. I've never found a four-leaf clover.

In conversation . . .

Responses in the present tense are the most common.

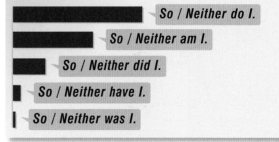

- So / Neither do I.
- So / Neither am I.
- So / Neither did I.
- So / Neither have I.
- So / Neither was I.

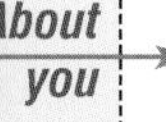

B ***Pair work*** Take turns making the sentences true for you and giving true responses.

"I don't think it's silly to be superstitious." ***"Neither do I."*** **or** ***"Actually, I think it is a bit silly."***

C ***Group work*** Do you believe in any superstitions? Tell the group. Are there any that you all have in common?

"I always make a wish when there's a full moon." ***"So do I, if I remember."***

5 Vocabulary notebook *Keep your fingers crossed.*

See page 62 for a useful way to log and learn vocabulary.

Lesson C Weird and off the wall

1 Conversation strategy *Making your meaning clear*

A How many different ways does this person say his friend is odd? Find the words he uses.

"One of my friends is kind of odd. I mean, she's nice and everything, but she's just a bit weird sometimes. You know, she says some strange things, so people think she's kind of funny."

Now listen to Carlos and Nicole. What does Nicole say about her dreams?

Carlos ***You look tired. Are you OK?***

Nicole ***Yeah, I'm fine. I guess I just had a bad night. I often don't sleep too well. You know, I have some strange dreams.***

Carlos ***You do? I hardly ever dream.***

Nicole ***Yeah. I, um . . . I've had some weird dreams. Really weird dreams. And they're scary. They're always scary ones. They're never good ones. They're just weird and off the wall.***

Carlos ***Like nightmares?***

Nicole ***Yeah. I have really bad nightmares. And I tend to have dreams that come true every once in a while. I try to be careful. You know the saying, "Don't tell a bad dream before breakfast because it might come true"?***

Carlos ***Never heard that. So, you tell it after breakfast?***

Nicole ***Yeah. Or sometimes not at all.***

Notice **how Nicole repeats her ideas to make her meaning clear. Sometimes she repeats the same words, and sometimes she uses different words. Find examples in the conversation.**

"I've had some weird dreams. Really weird dreams."

"They're always scary ones. They're never good ones."

B Complete each sentence by using a word from the list to repeat the main idea. Then discuss the statements with a partner. Do you agree with them?

1. Nightmares can be very scary, you know. They can be really ________ .
2. I think other people's dreams are really interesting. Really ________ .
3. Dreams have no meaning. They're just weird, ________ thoughts.
4. Insomnia must be awful. I mean, not being able to sleep must be ________ .
5. Most kids are afraid of the dark at some point. They all get ________ .
6. Sleepwalking is pretty common. It's nothing ________ .

crazy
fascinating
frightening
scared
terrible
unusual

2 Strategy plus *just*

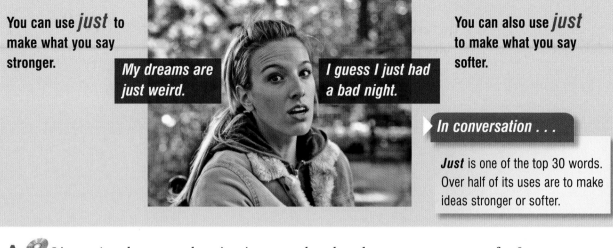

You can use *just* to make what you say stronger.

My dreams are just weird.

I guess I just had a bad night.

You can also use *just* to make what you say softer.

In conversation . . .

Just is one of the top 30 words. Over half of its uses are to make ideas stronger or softer.

A Listen. Are these people using *just* to make what they say stronger or softer? Check (✓) the boxes.

	Stronger	Softer
1. I often think about people, and then they call me. It's just amazing.	✓	☐
2. I just love all those TV shows about telepathy. They're fascinating.	✓	☐
3. I don't believe people can read minds. I just think they make good guesses.	☐	✓
4. I believe you can make wishes come true. You just have to try.	✓	☐
5. I don't think it's possible to hypnotize people. I just don't believe you can.	✓	☐
6. I don't think people who believe in UFOs are crazy. I think they just have active imaginations.	☐	✓

About you → **B Pair work** Are any of the sentences true for you? Tell a partner.

"I often think about people, and then I see them or they call. But I think it's just a coincidence."

3 Speaking naturally *Stressing new information*

*Nicole I have some strange **dreams**. . . . some **weird** dreams. **Really** weird dreams. And they're **scary**. They're **always** scary.*

A Listen and repeat what Nicole says about her dreams. Notice how the new information in each sentence gets the strongest stress.

B Can you predict which words have the strongest stress in the conversation below? Underline one word in each sentence. Then listen and check. Practice the conversation with a partner, and use your own information.

A ***Do you ever have bad dreams?***
B ***You mean scary dreams? Like nightmares?***
A ***Yeah. Dreams that make you all upset.***
B ***No. I usually have nice dreams. Fun dreams. What about you?***
A ***Oh, I never dream. At least, I never remember my dreams.***

An amazing story . . .

1 Reading

A Have you ever known any identical twins? How were they alike? Tell the class.

B Read the title of the article and the summary. What's the story about? Predict two things you think will happen in the story.

Separated **at birth . . .** by J.D. Heyman

Tamara Rabi and Adriana Scott

Growing up, they had a weird feeling something was missing. Turned out that "something" was their long-lost twin. After constantly mistaking one for the other, friends put two and two together and arranged a reunion.

Within weeks of showing up for her freshman year at Long Island's Hofstra University in New York, strange things started happening to Tamara Rabi. Strangers would smile and wave at her, then walk away peeved when she told them she didn't know them. "They must have thought I was crazy," says Rabi, 20. "Sometimes they'd ask me, 'Do you have a twin sister?' And I'd say 'No.'"

Just down the road at Adelphi University, Adriana Scott kept hearing similar questions about her dead ringer* at Hofstra. Nudged by friends, the young women got in touch by e-mail and discovered they both had been born in Guadalajara, Mexico, and adopted. Then Adriana's mother, Diana Scott, dropped a bombshell: When she and her late husband Peter, a vice president at a moving company, adopted her, they knew she had a twin who at the time was unavailable for adoption. Adriana's discovery "was a moment I'd dreaded for 20 years," says Diana, a receptionist.

While the Scotts raised Adriana in the Long Island suburbs, Tamara's adoptive parents, Yitzhak and Judy Rabi, who didn't know she was a twin, brought her up in Manhattan. "My family was very cautious," says Tamara, who learned about Adriana shortly after Yitzhak had died at age 58. "Even after they saw her photo, they had doubts. I was, like, 'C'mon, guys, the picture looks exactly like me!'"

Late last year, the girls agreed to meet on neutral ground at a local McDonald's and discovered that practically the only noticeable difference between them was a small birthmark above Tamara's right eyebrow. "Her voice was what got me," says Adriana. "I just sat there in shock." Even their mothers had trouble telling them apart.

Since then, the reunited twins and their widowed moms have formed a close bond, and recently they took a spa vacation together at a plush resort. "Tamara's sister could have been anyone in the world, but it turned out to be this wonderful girl," says Judy, 56. Adds Tamara: "It's like I'm starting a whole new life. For 20 years I haven't had a sister, and now I do."

**dead ringer* someone who looks identical to someone else

Source: *People* magazine

C Now read the article. Answer the questions. Were your predictions correct?

1. How did Tamara and Adriana get to know each other?
2. How are Tamara and Adriana alike? How are they different?
3. Have you ever heard of a story similar to theirs?

D ***Pair work*** Find these words and expressions in the article. Can you figure out their meaning from the context? Match each expression with a similar expression on the right.

1. put two and two together __g.__
2. showing up __b__
3. peeved __a.__
4. nudged __e__
5. dropped a bombshell __h.__
6. dreaded __f.__
7. on neutral ground __i__
8. telling them apart __d.__
9. formed a close bond __c__

a. annoyed
b. arriving
c. developed a good relationship
d. knowing who is who
e. encouraged
f. feared
g. figured something out
h. gave shocking news
i. at a place neither person knows well

2 Speaking and writing *Family stories*

A ***Group work*** Do you have any amazing stories to tell about your family? Discuss the questions.

- What's your family's background and history? Does your family have an interesting story?
- How did your parents meet? How about your grandparents?
- Is there anyone in your family you don't see very often? Why?
- Has your family ever had a family reunion? What was it like?
- Are you close to one particular member of your family? How did you become close?

B Choose one of the topics above, and write a story to share with the class.

Document 1

A true romance . . .

Before starting college, my mother had never ridden a bicycle in her life. Soon after arriving on campus, however, she met a guy who was the president of the college cycling club, and he invited her to join. My mother became a member of the club and bought a new bike.

The next weekend, she showed up at the group meeting with her new bicycle, and she was very surprised. She hadn't realized it was a racing club and that everyone had racing bikes. Her new bike was big and heavy, and it had a huge basket for shopping and books. She almost turned around and left after seeing all the professional-looking cyclists, but the club president persuaded her to stay. He rode with her – at the back.

To make a long story short, this guy ended up marrying my mother. He's my father, and he and my mother still love to go cycling together.

Help note

Prepositional time clauses

Notice in the sentences below, ***she*** is the subject of both verbs.

__Before starting__ college, she had never ridden a bicycle. = "Before she started college, she had never ridden a bicycle."

__Soon after arriving__ on campus, she met a guy. = "Soon after she arrived on campus, she met a guy."

She almost left __after seeing__ all the other cyclists. = "She almost left after she saw the other cyclists."

C ***Class activity*** Read your classmates' stories. Which story interests you the most?

3 Free talk *Can you believe it?*

See ***Free talk 6*** for more speaking practice.

Vocabulary notebook

Keep your fingers crossed.

Learning tip Grouping vocabulary

A good way to learn sayings, like proverbs or superstitions, is to group them according to topics, using word webs.

Good luck!

Over 50% of the uses of the word ***luck*** are when people talk about or wish others ***Good luck!***

Less than 5% of its uses are to talk about ***dumb***, ***bad***, ***poor***, ***tough***, or ***rotten luck***.

P. 56

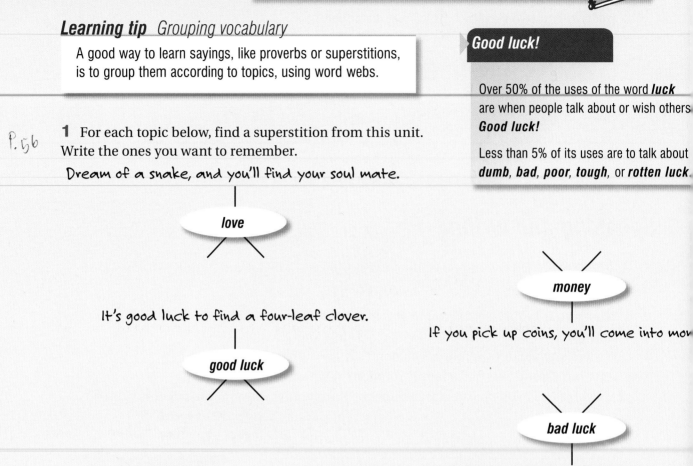

1 For each topic below, find a superstition from this unit. Write the ones you want to remember.

Dream of a snake, and you'll find your soul mate.

If you pick up coins, you'll come into mon

It's good luck to find a four-leaf clover.

If you break a mirror, you'll have seven years of bad luck.

2 ***Word builder*** Can you complete these superstitions? If you don't know them, you can look up the phrases in quotation marks (" ") in a search engine on the Internet. Then add them to the word webs above.

Finding a ladybug . . .
If you open an umbrella indoors, . . . badluck
Cut your nails on Friday, . . . sorrow

Bringing a new broom into a new house . . .
Putting clothes on with your left arm first . . . Unluc
Leave a house by the same door . . . good luck

On your own

Ask 5 people if they are superstitious about anything. Translate their superstitions into English.

Touchstone checkpoint Units 4–6

1 What are you supposed to do?

What do these signs mean? Write one or two sentences for each sign using *supposed to* or *not supposed to*. Compare with a partner. Where might you see these signs?

1 
2 
3 
4 
5 

A This one means you're not supposed to use your cell phone. You're supposed to turn it off.
B Yeah. You're supposed to turn cell phones off in hospitals, I think. And on planes.

2 You can say that again!

A Can you complete the second sentence so that it repeats the main idea of the first sentence? Add *just* to make the meaning stronger or softer. Compare with a partner.

1. I really enjoy going to parties. I just love going to parties.
2. I sometimes get a bit nervous when I meet new people. I just get . . . .
3. I don't go out every night because it's too expensive. It's just too expensive.
4. I'm never on time when I have to meet friends. I'm just never on time when I have . . . .

B Make the sentences true for you. Tell a partner your sentences. Use statement questions to check that you understand your partner's sentences.

A I really don't enjoy going to parties. I just hate being with a lot of people.
B Really? So you prefer to stay home?

3 Crime doesn't pay.

A How many ways can you complete the sentences below? Make true sentences.

	Crime		Punishment		Criminals		Punishment
People who are convicted of	shoplifting	usually get	fined.	I think	shoplifters	should be	fined.
	murder				murderer		

B Pair work Organize and explain your views. Say when your partner makes a good point.

A People who are convicted of shoplifting usually get fined. I think shoplifters should be fined. First, because it's not a really serious crime, and second, . . .
B That's a good point. But I think sometimes shoplifters should be sent to jail. For repeat offenses, or when they steal something really expensive.

4 A weird week

A Read the story and answer the questions below. Use the past perfect in your answers.

Last week, Eric had some bad luck and some good luck. Monday was a bad day. First, he saw a crow on his car when he left for work. After work, he went shopping with his girlfriend. She spent all her money on an expensive sweater, so he had to buy them both dinner. In the restaurant, Eric yelled at her for spending so much money, and she got very angry. On Tuesday, Eric bought her a gift to apologize – some sneakers – but she was still mad, and on Wednesday, she broke up with him.

On Thursday, Eric had a strange dream about a snake winding itself tightly around his leg. He didn't sleep well and overslept on Friday morning. He got dressed in a hurry and accidentally put his sweater on inside out. Later, while he was waiting in line at the bank, a woman behind him said, "Excuse me. Your sweater is inside out." He turned around and realized she was his old college friend, Sarah. He hadn't seen her since their graduation six years ago. What a nice surprise! Eric remembered his dream and suddenly thought, "This is the woman I'm going to marry."

1. Why did Eric have to pay for his girlfriend's dinner?
2. Why did Eric want to apologize?
3. Why did he oversleep on Friday morning?
4. Why was his sweater inside out?
5. Why was it a surprise to see Sarah?
6. Why did Eric have that last thought?

"Eric had to pay for his girlfriend's dinner because she had spent all her money on a sweater."

B ***Pair work*** Look at the superstitions on page 56. How might a superstitious person explain the events in the story? How many superstitions can you use? Discuss your ideas.

"Maybe Eric had a bad day on Monday because he'd seen a crow in the morning."

5 Get this!

Fill in the blanks with the correct forms of the *get* expressions in the box. Then practice.

get around to	get over	get through
✓get it	get the feeling	get used to

Ann My sister and her boyfriend just broke up. She's so upset.
Bill I don't __________. They were the perfect couple.
Ann I __________ that she was expecting it. She'll __________ it soon.
Bill Did they ever get engaged? Or didn't they __________ it?
Ann They did, but she'll soon __________ being single again.
Bill It's a tough time, but she'll __________ it.

6 Things in common?

Complete the sentences and compare with a partner. Say if you are the same or different. If you are the same, use *So* or *Neither*.

I believe in . . .	I don't believe in . . .	I was going to . . .
Once I tried . . .	I'm not a fan of . . .	I'm not supposed to . . .

"I believe in UFOs." "So do I. I think I saw one once."

Self-check

How sure are you about these ar
Circle the percentages.

grammar
20% 40% 60% 80% 100%
vocabulary
20% 40% 60% 80% 100%
conversation strategies
20% 40% 60% 80% 100%

Study plan

What do you want to review?
Circle the lessons.

grammar
4A 4B 5A 5B 6A 6B
vocabulary
4A 4B 5A 5B 6A 6B
conversation strategies
4C 5C 6C

Free talk 1 An interview with . . .

1 Choose a classmate to interview for an article in a magazine, and think of interesting things to ask him or her. Complete the questions below.

Questions for:	***Answers***
1. How long have you been ____________________ ?	____________
2. When did you last ____________________ ?	____________
3. Have you ever considered ____________________ ?	____________
4. What's your favorite ____________________ ?	____________
5. Have you ever tried ____________________ ?	____________
6. Where do you hope you'll ____________________ ?	____________
7. What do you like to ____________________ ?	____________
8. What's the nicest ____________________ ?	____________
9. Who do you ____________________ ?	____________
10. What do you remember about ____________________ ?	____________
11. What were you doing ____________________ ?	____________
12. How did you end up ____________________ ?	____________

2 ***Pair work*** Now ask your interview questions. Take notes on your partner's answers.

3 ***Class activity*** Share the most interesting questions and answers with the class.

Free talk 2 What's popular?

Group work Discuss the questions. Do you agree on your answers?

1. Which cars are popular right now? What kind of car would you like to own? Why?
2. What clothing styles are in fashion right now? Do you like the new styles as much as last year's styles?
3. Which hairstyles are trendy now? How have they changed over the last couple of years? Has your own hairstyle changed?
4. What bands are popular right now? Are there any bands that you don't hear about as much as you used to?
5. Are there any diets or kinds of food that are popular? Is your diet as healthy as it could be?
6. What kinds of exercise are popular?
7. How have your personal tastes changed over the last five years – for example, in fashion, music, and food?
8. What do you like now that you didn't like two years ago?

A ***Well, those big SUVs are popular right now. It seems like you see them everywhere.***

B ***Right. I'm not sure I'd like to own one, though. They're not as economical as a car.***

C ***That's true. But don't you think it would be fun to drive one?***

Local customs

1 ***Pair work*** Plan a presentation on local customs for visitors to your country, or another country that you both know about. Use the topics below to give you ideas, and add more of your own.

Greeting people

Eating traditional food

Visiting someone's home

Shopping

2 ***Class activity*** Now take turns making your presentations. As you listen to each one, write down one piece of information that you think visitors will find particularly useful. Be sure to ask questions at the end if you didn't hear or understand something properly.

"Welcome to Brazil. If you are visiting our country, there are some useful things you need to know about our local customs. Brazilian people are very friendly, and they always greet you with a warm smile. . . ."

Free talk 4 Pass on the message.

Class activity You are going to play a message game. Follow the instructions below step-by-step.

Step 1 Write your name on a piece of paper, fold it, and put it on your teacher's desk. Then pick another piece of paper from the pile. Read the name on the paper, but keep it a secret.

Step 2 Think of a place you would like to go with the person whose name you picked. Complete the chart with information about your plans.

a place you would like to go	
what day	
what the event is supposed to be like	
a time and place to meet	
what to wear	
how much it costs	
one thing to bring along	
what the weather is supposed to be like	

Step 3 Ask another classmate to pass on the message to the person whose name you picked. Explain the details of your invitation.

"Could you pass on a message to Pablo? Tell him I'd like to go to the movies with him tonight. There's a new action movie playing at the Roxy, and it's supposed to be really good. Tell him to meet me at 6:00 at . . ."

Step 4 Another classmate will tell you a message to pass on to someone else. Listen carefully and try to remember all the details.

Step 5 Pass on the message that you were told. Did you remember everything?

Step 6 Someone else will pass on a message to you. Listen carefully for all the details. Then consider the invitation. Do you want to accept? Are you free? Tell the class.

"Carla asked me to go to a concert tomorrow night. It's a jazz group, and they're supposed to be really good. We're supposed to meet at 7:00 at the concert hall. Jeans are OK, and tickets cost $10. I should bring an umbrella because it's supposed to rain. But unfortunately, I can't go. I'm supposed to be going out with my sister tomorrow night. . . ."

Step 7 When the person you invited out tells the class about your invitation, check the information in your chart. How well did your messenger pass on your message?

Free talk 5 Lawmakers

1 *Pair work* Imagine you are on a committee that proposes new laws to the government. Choose one of the topic areas below. Think of reasons for and against each of these possible new laws.

Marriage vows People shouldn't be allowed . . .

- to get married until they have taken a marriage-preparation course.
- to get a divorce until they have been married for 10 years.
- to marry before the age of 21.

Education A law should be passed . . .

- that prohibits students from quitting school before the age of 18.
- to make everyone learn at least two foreign languages.
- to ban examinations for students under 16.

Driving A law should be passed . . .

- to prevent people over 70 from driving a vehicle.
- to ban high fees for car insurance for young people.
- to stop companies from making cars that go faster than the speed limit.

2 *Group work* Find another pair who chose the same topic as you. Compare your arguments for and against the laws. Which laws do you agree to propose to the government? Which do you decide to drop?

Free talk 6 Can you believe it?

Pair work Take turns telling each other about these unusual beliefs and strange events.

Can you think of . . .

1. *something you used to believe as a child but you don't believe now?*
2. *something you are superstitious about?*
3. *something that happened to you that was really good luck?*
4. *a time when you dreamed about something and then it came true?*
5. *a time when you were able to tell what someone else was thinking?*
6. *a time when you experienced a strange coincidence?*

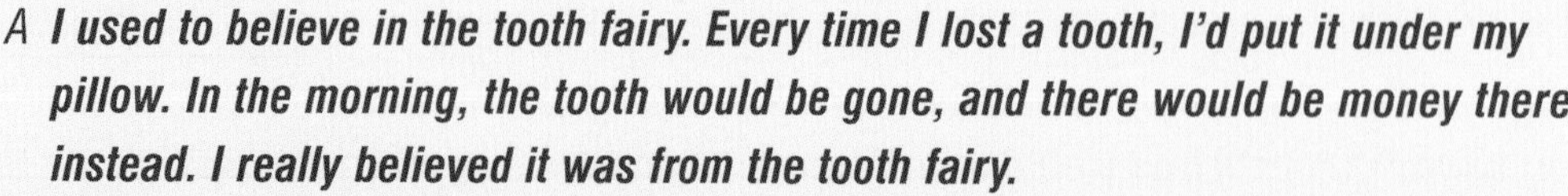

A ***I used to believe in the tooth fairy. Every time I lost a tooth, I'd put it under my pillow. In the morning, the tooth would be gone, and there would be money there instead. I really believed it was from the tooth fairy.***

B ***I did too. I didn't realize it was my parents who gave me the money until I was about ten. And I was so disappointed!***

Self-study listening

Unit 1

A *Track 1* Listen to the conversation on page 6. Juan and Bryan are telling Kim a story.

B *Track 2* Listen to the rest of their conversation. Check (✓) true or false for each sentence.

	True	False
1. *Juan and Bryan saw a bear.*	☐	☐
2. *Kim's story is about a time she was camping.*	☐	☐
3. *Kim was eating dinner when she heard the noise.*	☐	☐
4. *Kim didn't have any food in the tent.*	☐	☐
5. *Kim decided that if she saw a bear, she would run.*	☐	☐
6. *A bear was looking for something to eat.*	☐	☐

Unit 2

A *Track 3* Listen to the conversation on page 16. Tracy and Omar are shopping for a birthday gift.

B *Track 4* Listen to the rest of their conversation. Circle the correct words.

1. ***Tracy* / *Tracy's sister*** *subscribes to music magazines.*
2. *Tracy's sister* ***has* / *doesn't have*** *broad tastes in music.*
3. *Tracy's sister and Omar's brother like* ***the same* / *different*** *kinds of music.*
4. *Omar thinks his brother and Tracy's sister* ***would* / *wouldn't*** *like each other.*
5. *Tracy* ***is* / *isn't*** *invited to the party.*

Unit 3

A *Track 5* Listen to the conversation on page 26. Hilda and David are talking in the classroom.

B *Track 6* Listen to the rest of their conversation. Choose the right answer. Circle ***a*** or ***b***.

1. *What does David think Hilda should do?*
   a. *Travel in the U.S.*
   b. *Study in the U.S.*
2. *How long would Hilda like to be away?*
   a. *For the summer.*
   b. *For a year.*
3. *When does Hilda need to apply by?*
   a. *The end of the month.*
   b. *The beginning of the summer.*
4. *Who should Hilda talk to?*
   a. *Another teacher.*
   b. *Another student.*
5. *What does she have to send in with her application?*
   a. *A teacher recommendation and an essay.*
   b. *A teacher recommendation and some money.*

Unit 4

A *Track 7* Listen to the conversation on page 38. Grant and Martin are talking about surprise parties.

B *Track 8* Listen to the rest of their conversation. Check (✓) true or false for each sentence.

	True	False
1. *Grant was supposed to organize a surprise party for Martin.*	☐	☐
2. *Martin was planning to work late on his birthday.*	☐	☐
3. *Grant has already booked a band for the party.*	☐	☐
4. *Martin likes the band that's supposed to play at his party.*	☐	☐
5. *Martin wants Grant to cancel the party.*	☐	☐

Unit 5

A *Track 9* Listen to the conversation on page 48. Jin Ho and Celia are talking about security cameras.

B *Track 10* Listen to the rest of their conversation. Circle the correct words.

1. *Jin Ho says a lot of people* ***don't know about / don't like*** *the cameras.*
2. *Celia thinks speeders should be* ***punished / given a second chance****.*
3. *The fine for speeding is* ***$60 / $600****.*
4. *Jin Ho* ***has already paid / is going to pay*** *the fine.*
5. *Jin Ho agrees that speed cameras* ***work / don't work*** *as a deterrent.*
6. *Jin Ho needs Celia to* ***lend him some money / give him a ride****.*

Unit 6

A *Track 11* Listen to the conversation on page 58. Carlos is asking Nicole about her bad dreams.

B *Track 12* Listen to the rest of their conversation. Complete the sentences. Circle ***a*** or ***b***.

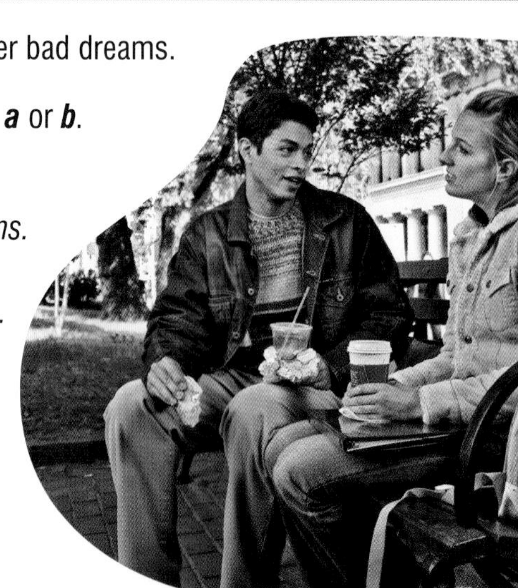

1. *Carlos says your sleep is affected by . . .*
   - a. *the direction your bed faces.*
   - b. *the room you sleep in.*
2. *Nicole can't move her bed because . . .*
   - a. *it's too heavy.*
   - b. *it won't fit anywhere else.*
3. *Some people believe bad dreams . . .*
   - a. *come in through windows.*
   - b. *come in through doors.*
4. *Dream catchers are . . .*
   - a. *people who have bad dreams.*
   - b. *window decorations.*
5. *Carlos saw dream catchers . . .*
   - a. *in a friend's room.*
   - b. *in stores.*
6. *Nicole is planning to . . .*
   - a. *buy a dream catcher.*
   - b. *make a dream catcher.*

Unit 1

Kim That's so funny! What did you think the noise was?
Bryan I don't know. We didn't bother to find out! Maybe a bear?
Juan I just remember running because Bryan started running.
Kim I almost saw a bear once. Sort of.
Bryan What do you mean?
Kim I was camping with my family. And one night, my sister and I were in our tent, just going to sleep, and suddenly we hear this noise outside. There was something walking around the campsite, knocking things over.
Juan Oh, no!
Kim So my sister goes, "It's a bear. It's looking for food," and then she says, "I'm glad we don't have any food in here."
Bryan Yeah. Bears can rip right through a tent if they smell food.
Kim I know! But then I had to tell my sister that I actually had some candy bars with me. So now we're both terrified. And we decide to look outside the tent and run if we see a bear!
Juan So? What was it?
Kim Something looking for food, all right, but it was my dad!

Unit 2

Tracy A magazine subscription's a really nice gift.
Omar Yeah. I wonder which one to get, though.
Tracy You know, my sister gets music magazines – *Music Monthly*, *Music News*, *Pop World*. I could ask her which one's the best.
Omar OK. That'd be great. Now, what kind of music is she into?
Tracy Oh, all kinds of stuff. Hip-hop, soft rock, soul, classical, . . .
Omar Pretty much everything, then. Sounds like she likes music as much as my brother does.
Tracy Yeah. And the same kinds of music, too.
Omar You know, maybe we should get them together sometime. Don't you think they'd get along?
Tracy Oh, yeah. Definitely. They've got a lot in common.
Omar Maybe I should invite her to my brother's birthday party.
Tracy Great idea. She'd love it. She's pretty outgoing, you know.
Omar OK. I'll send her an invitation.
Tracy Um . . . what about me? Aren't you inviting me, too?
Omar You? Yes, I'm inviting you! You chose his gift, after all!

Unit 3

Hilda It sounds like you really love it here.
David I do. You know, you should think about spending a year at school in the U.S. I think you'd enjoy living there.
Hilda Oh, I don't know. To tell you the truth, I think it would be hard to be away from my family for so long.
David Of course. Well, maybe you'd like to go for a shorter time. Many universities offer summer programs, you know.
Hilda Going away just for the summer sounds better. I'd like that.
David In fact, there's still time to apply for this summer. You just need to mail your application by the end of the month.
Hilda This summer? Really? Well, I don't have any plans yet. . . .
David Do you know Patricia in my Monday class? She's going to study in New York this summer. You should talk to her.
Hilda I will. What else do I have to send in with the application?
David An essay and a recommendation from your English teacher.
Hilda OK. Well, would you be able to check my essay . . . and maybe write a recommendation for me, too?
David Of course I would! I'd be happy to help.

Unit 4

Grant So, you really don't like surprise parties, huh?
Martin No, I don't. Why? Wait a minute – are you planning one?
Grant Well, I was supposed to. We were going to do something for you after work, but if you really don't like the idea, . . .
Martin I'd rather not. I was just going to get off work a bit early and have a quiet evening with a couple of friends. Have you already made all the arrangements and everything?
Grant Well, just a few, like we booked the place and invited people, and Brad was going to book a band. But I don't know if he got around to doing that, so . . .
Martin Huh. Which band?
Grant It's a local band – The Beat. They're supposed to be good.
Martin You're kidding! The Beat? They're excellent. I really like them. Well, you guys probably can't get out of that. . . .
Grant I don't know. We might be able to . . .
Martin Well, wait. I think I like the sound of this surprise party.
Grant Yeah? So, do I get the feeling we should go ahead with it?
Martin Oh, sure. I'm looking forward to it now. The Beat . . . cool!

Unit 5

Jin Ho Another thing is, a lot of people don't know the cameras are there – like speed cameras on the highway.
Celia Yeah, but I don't have a problem with speed cameras. For two reasons – number one, speeding is dangerous. That's just a fact. And, two, it's against the law. If people get caught speeding, they should be punished.
Jin Ho Well, yeah, that's true. But the point is, people ought to be told where the cameras are. And secondly, they should be told it's a $600 fine if they get caught.
Celia Well, you've got a point there. Wow. $600 is expensive! I had no idea. So how do you know how much the fine is?
Jin Ho Well, uh, I got caught last month. And I just paid the fine. I won't get caught speeding again, that's for sure!
Celia So you see, those cameras *do* work! They *are* a deterrent.
Jin Ho Yeah, that's true. Anyway, would you mind giving me a ride home later? I can't afford to drive for a while.

Unit 6

Carlos Maybe you should change the position of your bed.
Nicole Why? How would that help?
Carlos Well, I've heard that if you sleep with your head to the north, you won't sleep well.
Nicole Really? Who told you that?
Carlos My aunt. She'd always been a terrible sleeper, but when she changed her bed to face east, she slept fine.
Nicole I can't change the position of my bed. My room has a lot of windows, so I can't put my bed against another wall.
Carlos Maybe *that's* the problem! Some Native Americans believe that bad dreams come in through your windows.
Nicole They do? Well, I can't get rid of my windows!
Carlos No, but you could put a dream catcher in a window. You've seen dream catchers, right? They're made of feathers and string and stuff. I've seen them in stores.
Nicole So have I. Huh. Do you think it would work?
Carlos Well, it might. They're supposed to catch the bad dreams before they reach you. And I think they look cool.
Nicole So do I. OK. I'll get one and try it tonight.

Answer key

Unit 1 1. False 2. True 3. False 4. False 5. True 6. False
Unit 2 1. Tracy's sister 2. has 3. the same 4. would 5. is
Unit 3 1. b 2. a 3. a 4. b 5. a
Unit 4 1. True 2. False 3. False 4. True 5. False
Unit 5 1. don't know about 2. punished 3. $600 4. has already paid 5. work 6. give him a ride
Unit 6 1. a 2. b 3. a 4. b 5. b 6. a

Illustration credits

Lisa Blackshear: 54
Frank Montagna: 7, 24, 41, FT-D (*bottom*)
Marilena Perilli: viii, 14, 31, 36, 47, 57
Greg White: 10, 20, 30, 42, 52, 62
Terry Wong: 13
Filip Yip: 17

Photography credits

6, 7, 12, 16, 17, 18, 26, 27, 38, 39, 48, 49 (*top*), **58, 59, SSL1, SSL2,** ©Frank Veronsky
1 (*clockwise from top right*) ©Don Mason/Corbis; ©Owen Franken/Corbis; ©Peter Beavis/Getty Images; ©Tim Hall/Getty Images
2 ©Randy Faris/Corbis
3 ©Camelot/Getty Images
4 ©Punchstock
8 ©Mark Richards
9 ©Armando Franca/AP/Wide World
11 (*clockwise from top right*) ©Punchstock; ©Digital Vision/Getty Images; ©Motoring Picture Library/Alamy; ©Digital Vision/Getty Images
21 (*clockwise from top right*) ©AFP/Getty Images; ©Angelo Cavalli/Getty Images; ©Photos.com; ©China Photos/Stringer/Getty Images; ©Age fotostock; ©Stewart Cohen/Getty Images
22 (*top, left to right*) ©Punchstock; ©Alamy; ©Danita Delimont/Alamy; ©David South/Alamy; (*bottom, left to right*) ©Alamy; ©Dave Bartruff/Corbis; ©Vidler/Age fotostock; ©Andy Caulfield/Getty Images
25 ©Index Stock
32 ©Jupiter Images
33 (*clockwise from top right*) ©Wendell Metzen/Index Stock; ©Juan Silva/Getty Images; ©Punchstock; ©Punchstock
34 (*top, left to right*) ©Punchstock; ©Punchstock; ©Getty Images; ©Punchstock; (*bottom, left to right*) ©Punchstock; ©Imageshop/Alamy; ©Punchstock; ©Getty Images
35 ©Punchstock
43 (*clockwise from top left*) ©Corbis; ©Punchstock; ©R. Ian Lloyd/Masterfile
44 (*top, left to right*) ©Punchstock; ©Corbis; (*bottom, left to right*) ©Alamy; ©Getty Images; ©Corbis
49 (*bottom*) ©Punchstock
50 ©Paul Thomas/Getty Images
51 ©PR Newswire Photo Service/Newscom
53 (*clockwise from top right*) ©Jonathan Knowles/Getty Images; (*inset*) ©Punchstock; ©David Schmidt/Masterfile; ©Punchstock; ©Zefa/Corbis
54 (*both*) ©Punchstock
55 ©Corbis
56 (*left to right*) ©Pegaz/Alamy; ©Punchstock; ©Punchstock; ©Larry F. Jernigan /Index Stock
60 ©Angel Franco/The New York Times
FT-A (*top to bottom*) Courtesy of Mini USA; Courtesy of Toyota; Courtesy of Ford Motor Company
FT-B (*clockwise from top left*) ©Wide Group/Getty Images; ©Alamy; ©Michelle Garrett/Corbis; ©Getty Images; ©Heungman Kwan/Index Stock

Text credits

The authors and publishers are grateful for permission to reprint the following items:

8 Adapted from "Bad Idea. You'll Flunk Out" by Pat Galloway, *Time Magazine*. March 7, 2005. © 2005 Time Inc. All rights reserved. Reprinted with permission.
28 Adapted from "Counting Chickens – Milking Cats" by Fred D. Baldwin, *Attaché* magazine. October 2004. Reprinted by permission.
40 Adapted from "Socializing the introvert" by Jenny Yuen, *Toronto Observer*. October 23, 2002. Reprinted by permission.
50 Adapted from "Cam Phones, Go Home" by Carolina A. Miranda, *Time Magazine*. February 7, 2005. © 2005 Time Inc. All rights reserved. Reprinted with permission.
60 Adapted from "Separated at Birth: Tamara Rabi and Adriana Scott" by J.D. Heyman, *People* magazine. May 5, 2003. © 2003 Time Inc. All rights reserved. Reprinted by permission.

Every effort has been made to trace the owners of copyrighted material in this publication. We would be grateful to hear from anyone who recognizes his or her copyrighted material and who is unacknowledged. We will be pleased to make the necessary corrections in future editions.